AWS Greengrass Developer Guide

A catalogue record for this book is available from the Hong Kong Public Libraries.

Published in Hong Kong by Samurai Media Limited.

Email: info@samuraimedia.org

ISBN 9789888408467

Contents

What Is AWS Greengrass?

AWS Greengrass is software that extends AWS cloud capabilities to local devices, making it possible for them to collect and analyze data closer to the source of information, while also securely communicating with each other on local networks. More specifically, developers who use AWS Greengrass can author serverless code (AWS Lambda functions) in the cloud and conveniently deploy it to devices for local execution of applications.

The following diagram shows the basic architecture of AWS Greengrass.

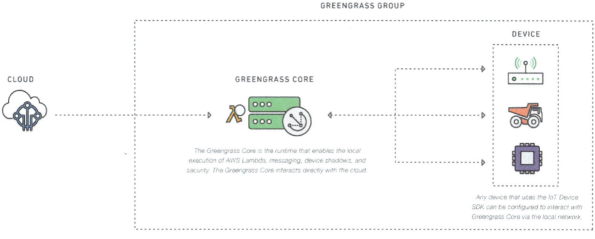

A defined group of Greengrass Cores and other devices that are configured to communicate with one another. A Greengrass Group may represent one floor of a building, one truck, or one home.

AWS Greengrass makes it possible for customers to use Lambda functions to build IoT devices and application logic. Specifically, AWS Greengrass provides cloud-based management of applications that can be deployed for local execution. Locally deployed Lambda functions are triggered by local events, messages from the cloud, or other sources.

In AWS Greengrass, devices securely communicate on a local network and exchange messages with each other without having to connect to the cloud. AWS Greengrass provides a local pub/sub message manager that can intelligently buffer messages if connectivity is lost so that inbound and outbound messages to the cloud are preserved.

AWS Greengrass protects user data:

- Through the secure authentication and authorization of devices.
- Through secure connectivity in the local network.
- Between local devices and the cloud.

Device security credentials function within a group until they are revoked, even if connectivity to the cloud is disrupted, so that the devices can continue to securely communicate locally.

AWS Greengrass provides secure, over-the-air software updates of Lambda functions.

AWS Greengrass consists of:

- Software distributions
    - AWS Greengrass core software
    - AWS Greengrass core SDK
- Cloud service
    - AWS Greengrass API
- Features
    - Lambda runtime
    - Shadows implementation

- Message manager
- Group management
- Discovery service
- Over-the-air update agent
- Local resource access
- Machine learning inference

AWS Greengrass Core Software

The AWS Greengrass Core software provides the following functionality:

- Allows deployment and execution of local applications created using Lambda functions and managed through the deployment API.
- Enables local messaging between devices over a secure network using a managed subscription scheme through the MQTT protocol.
- Ensures secure connections between devices and the cloud using device authentication and authorization.
- Provides secure, over-the-air software updates of user-defined Lambda functions.

The AWS Greengrass Core software consists of:

- A message manager that routes messages between devices, Lambda functions, and AWS IoT.
- A Lambda runtime that runs user-defined Lambda functions.
- An implementation of the Device Shadow service that provides a local copy of shadows, which represent your devices. Shadows can be configured to sync with the cloud.
- A deployment agent that is notified of new or updated AWS Greengrass group configuration. When new or updated configuration is detected, the deployment agent downloads the configuration data and restarts the AWS Greengrass core.

AWS Greengrass core instances are configured through AWS Greengrass APIs that create and update AWS Greengrass group definitions stored in the cloud.

AWS Greengrass core versions:

[GGC v1.5.0]

Current version.

New features:

- AWS Greengrass Machine Learning (ML) Inference is generally available. You can perform ML inference locally on AWS Greengrass devices using models that are built and trained in the cloud. For more information, see Perform Machine Learning Inference.
- Greengrass Lambda functions now support binary data as their input payload, in addition to JSON. To use this feature, you must upgrade to AWS Greengrass Core SDK version 1.1.0, which you can download from the **Software** page in the AWS IoT console.

Bug fixes and improvements:

- Reduced the overall memory footprint.
- Performance improvements for sending messages to the cloud.
- Performance and stability improvements for the download agent, Device Certificate Manager, and OTA update agent.
- Minor bug fixes.

[GGC v1.3.0]

New features:

- Over-the-air (OTA) update agent capable of handling cloud-deployed, Greengrass update jobs. The agent is found under the new **/greengrass/ota** directory. For more information, see OTA Updates of AWS Greengrass Core Software.
- Local Resource Access feature allows Greengrass Lambda functions to access local resources, such as peripheral devices and volumes. For more information, see Access Local Resources with Lambda Functions.

[GGC v1.1.0]

To migrate from the previous version of the AWS Greengrass core:

- Copy certificates from the /greengrass/configuration/certs folder to /greengrass/certs
- Copy /greengrass/configuration/config.json to /greengrass/config/config.json
- Run /greengrass/ggc/core/greengrassd instead of /greengrass/greengrassd
- Deploy the group to the new core.

[GGC v1.0.0]

Initial version.

AWS Greengrass Groups

An AWS Greengrass group definition is a collection of settings for AWS Greengrass core devices and the devices that communicate with them. The following diagram shows the objects that make up an AWS Greengrass group.

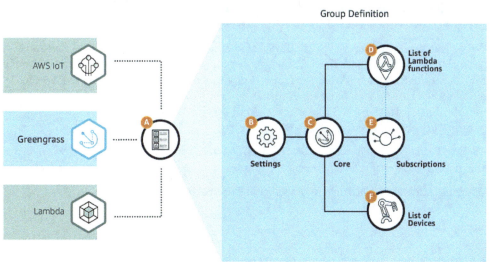

In the preceding diagram:

A: AWS Greengrass group definition
A collection of information about the AWS Greengrass group.

B: AWS Greengrass group settings
These include:

- AWS Greengrass group role.
- Log configuration.
- Certification authority and local connection configuration.
- AWS Greengrass core connectivity information.

C: AWS Greengrass core
The AWS IoT thing that represents the AWS Greengrass core.

D: Lambda function definition
A list of Lambda functions to be deployed to the AWS Greengrass core of the group.

E: Subscription definition
A collection of subscriptions to be deployed to the AWS Greengrass group that contains:

- A message rule ID, a unique identifier for the message routing subscription.
- A message source, an ARN that identifies the source of the message. Valid values are a thing ARN, Lambda function, or "cloud".
- A subject, an MQTT topic or topic filter used to filter message data.
- A target, an ARN that identifies the destination for messages published by the message source. Valid values are a thing ARN, Lambda function, or "cloud".

F: Device definition
A list containing an AWS Greengrass core and AWS IoT things that are members of the AWS Greengrass group and associated configuration data. This data specifies which devices are AWS Greengrass cores and which devices should sync shadow data with AWS IoT.

When deployed, the AWS Greengrass group definition, Lambda functions, and subscription table are copied to an AWS Greengrass core device.

Devices in AWS Greengrass

There are two types of devices:

- AWS Greengrass cores.
- AWS IoT devices connected to an AWS Greengrass core.

An AWS Greengrass core is an AWS IoT device that runs specialized AWS Greengrass software that communicates directly with the AWS IoT and AWS Greengrass cloud services. It is an AWS IoT device with its own certificate used for authenticating with AWS IoT. It has a device shadow and exists in the AWS IoT device registry. AWS Greengrass cores run a local Lambda runtime, a deployment agent, and an IP address tracker that sends IP address information to the AWS Greengrass cloud service to allow AWS IoT devices to automatically discover their group and core connection information.

Any AWS IoT device can connect to an AWS Greengrass core. An AWS Greengrass core runs software written with the AWS IoT Device SDK.

The following table shows how these device types are related.

	Core	Device
Certificate	✅	✅
IoT Policy	✅	✅
IoT Thing	✅	✅
Device use sample	Gateway	Sensor and/or Actuator
Software	Greengrass Core Software	AWS IoT Device SDK
Group membership	✅	✅
Functions outside an AWS Greengrass Group	❌	✅

The AWS Greengrass core device stores certificates in two locations:

- Core device certificate in /greengrass/certs - The core device certificate is named `hash.cert.pem`, for example `86c84488a5.cert.pem`. This certificate is used to authenticate the core when connecting to the AWS IoT and AWS Greengrass services.
- MQTT core server certificate in /greengrass/ggc/var/state/server - The MQTT core server certificate is named `server.crt`. This certificate is used for mutual authentication between the local MQTT service (that's on the Greengrass core) and Greengrass devices before messages are exchanged.

SDKs

The following SDKs are used when working with AWS Greengrass:

[**GGC v1.5.0**]

AWS SDKs
Using the AWS SDKs, you can build applications that work with any AWS service, including Amazon S3, Amazon DynamoDB, AWS IoT, AWS Greengrass, and more. In the context of AWS Greengrass, you can use the AWS SDK inside deployed Lambda functions to make direct calls to any AWS service.

AWS IoT Device SDKs
The AWS IoT Device SDKs helps devices connect to AWS IoT or AWS Greengrass services. Devices must know which AWS Greengrass group they belong to and the IP address of the AWS Greengrass core that they should

connect to.

Although you can use any of the AWS IoT Device SDKs to connect to an AWS Greengrass core, only the C++ and Python Device SDKs provide AWS Greengrass-specific functionality, such as access to the AWS Greengrass Discovery Service and AWS Greengrass core root CA downloads. For more information, see AWS IoT Device SDK.

AWS Greengrass Core SDK

The AWS Greengrass Core SDK enables Lambda functions to interact with the AWS Greengrass core on which they run in order to publish messages, interact with the local Device Shadow service, or invoke other deployed Lambda functions. This SDK is used exclusively for writing Lambda functions running in the Lambda runtime on an AWS Greengrass core. Lambda functions running on an AWS Greengrass core can interact with AWS cloud services directly using the AWS SDK. The AWS Greengrass Core SDK and the AWS SDK are contained in different packages, so you can use both packages simultaneously. You can download the AWS Greengrass Core SDK from the **Software** page of the AWS IoT console.

The AWS Greengrass Core SDK follows the AWS SDK programming model. It allows you to easily port Lambda functions developed for the cloud to Lambda functions that run on an AWS Greengrass core. For example, using the AWS SDK, the following Lambda function publishes a message to the topic `"/some/topic"` in the cloud:

```
1 import boto3
2
3 client = boto3.client('iot-data')
4 response = client.publish(
5     topic = "/some/topic",
6     qos = 0,
7     payload = "Some payload".encode()
8 )
```

To port this Lambda function for execution on an AWS Greengrass core, replace the `import boto3` statement with the `import greengrasssdk`, as shown in the following snippet:

The AWS Greengrass Core SDK only supports sending MQTT messages with QoS = 0.

```
1 import greengrasssdk
2
3 client = greengrasssdk.client('iot-data')
4 response = client.publish(
5     topic='/some/topic',
6     qos=0,
7     payload='some payload'.encode()
8 )
```

This allows you to test your Lambda functions in the cloud and migrate them to AWS Greengrass with minimal effort.

Note

The AWS SDK is natively part of the environment when executing a Lambda function in the AWS cloud. If you want to use `boto3` in a Lambda function deployed on an AWS Greengrass core, make sure to include the AWS SDK in your package. In addition, if you choose to use both the AWS Greengrass Core SDK and the AWS SDK simultaneously in the same package, your Lambda functions must use the correct namespace. For more information about how to create your deployment package, see:

AWS Lambda Creating a Deployment Package (Python) AWS Lambda Creating a Deployment Package (NodeJS) AWS Lambda Creating a Deployment Package (Java)

[**GGC v1.3.0**]

AWS SDKs

Using the AWS SDKs, you can build applications that work with any AWS service, including Amazon S3, Amazon DynamoDB, AWS IoT, AWS Greengrass, and more. In the context of AWS Greengrass, you can use the AWS SDK inside deployed Lambda functions to make direct calls to any AWS service.

AWS IoT Device SDKs

The AWS IoT Device SDKs helps devices connect to AWS IoT or AWS Greengrass services. Devices must know which AWS Greengrass group they belong to and the IP address of the AWS Greengrass core that they should connect to.

Although you can use any of the AWS IoT Device SDKs to connect to an AWS Greengrass core, only the C++ and Python Device SDKs provide AWS Greengrass-specific functionality, such as access to the AWS Greengrass Discovery Service and AWS Greengrass core root CA downloads. For more information, see AWS IoT Device SDK.

AWS Greengrass Core SDK

The AWS Greengrass Core SDK enables Lambda functions to interact with the AWS Greengrass core on which they run in order to publish messages, interact with the local Device Shadow service, or invoke other deployed Lambda functions. This SDK is used exclusively for writing Lambda functions running in the Lambda runtime on an AWS Greengrass core. Lambda functions running on an AWS Greengrass core can interact with AWS cloud services directly using the AWS SDK. The AWS Greengrass Core SDK and the AWS SDK are contained in different packages, so you can use both packages simultaneously. You can download the AWS Greengrass Core SDK from the **Software** page of the AWS IoT console.

The AWS Greengrass Core SDK follows the AWS SDK programming model. It allows you to easily port Lambda functions developed for the cloud to Lambda functions that run on an AWS Greengrass core. For example, using the AWS SDK, the following Lambda function publishes a message to the topic "/some/topic" in the cloud:

```
1  import boto3
2
3  client = boto3.client('iot-data')
4  response = client.publish(
5      topic = "/some/topic",
6      qos = 0,
7      payload = "Some payload".encode()
8  )
```

To port this Lambda function for execution on an AWS Greengrass core, replace the `import boto3` statement with the `import greengrasssdk`, as shown in the following snippet:

The AWS Greengrass Core SDK only supports sending MQTT messages with QoS = 0.

```
1  import greengrasssdk
2
3  client = greengrasssdk.client('iot-data')
4  response = client.publish(
5      topic='/some/topic',
6      qos=0,
7      payload='some payload'.encode()
8  )
```

This allows you to test your Lambda functions in the cloud and migrate them to AWS Greengrass with minimal effort.

Note

The AWS SDK is natively part of the environment when executing a Lambda function in the AWS cloud. If you want to use `boto3` in a Lambda function deployed on an AWS Greengrass core, make sure to include the AWS SDK in your package. In addition, if you choose to use both the AWS Greengrass Core SDK and the AWS SDK simultaneously in the same package, your Lambda functions must use the correct namespace. For more information about how to create your deployment package, see:

AWS Lambda Creating a Deployment Package (Python) AWS Lambda Creating a Deployment Package (NodeJS) AWS Lambda Creating a Deployment Package (Java)

[GGC v1.1.0]

AWS SDKs

Using the AWS SDKs, you can build applications that work with any AWS service, including Amazon S3, Amazon DynamoDB, AWS IoT, AWS Greengrass, and more. In the context of AWS Greengrass, you can use the AWS SDK inside deployed Lambda functions to make direct calls to any AWS service.

AWS IoT Device SDKs

The AWS IoT Device SDKs helps devices connect to AWS IoT or AWS Greengrass services. Devices must know which AWS Greengrass group they belong to and the IP address of the AWS Greengrass core that they should connect to.

Although you can use any of the AWS IoT Device SDKs to connect to an AWS Greengrass core, only the C++ and Python Device SDKs provide AWS Greengrass-specific functionality, such as access to the AWS Greengrass Discovery Service and AWS Greengrass core root CA downloads. For more information, see AWS IoT Device SDK.

AWS Greengrass Core SDK

The AWS Greengrass Core SDK enables Lambda functions to interact with the AWS Greengrass core on which they run in order to publish messages, interact with the local Device Shadow service, or invoke other deployed Lambda functions. This SDK is used exclusively for writing Lambda functions running in the Lambda runtime on an AWS Greengrass core. Lambda functions running on an AWS Greengrass core can interact with AWS cloud services directly using the AWS SDK. The AWS Greengrass Core SDK and the AWS SDK are contained in different packages, so you can use both packages simultaneously. You can download the AWS Greengrass Core SDK from the **Software** page of the AWS IoT console.

The AWS Greengrass Core SDK follows the AWS SDK programming model. It allows you to easily port Lambda functions developed for the cloud to Lambda functions that run on an AWS Greengrass core. For example, using the AWS SDK, the following Lambda function publishes a message to the topic "/some/topic" in the cloud:

```
1 import boto3
2
3 client = boto3.client('iot-data')
4 response = client.publish(
5     topic = "/some/topic",
6     qos = 0,
7     payload = "Some payload".encode()
8 )
```

To port this Lambda function for execution on an AWS Greengrass core, replace the `import boto3` statement with the `import greengrasssdk`, as shown in the following snippet:

The AWS Greengrass Core SDK only supports sending MQTT messages with QoS = 0.

```
1 import greengrasssdk
2
3 client = greengrasssdk.client('iot-data')
4 response = client.publish(
5     topic='/some/topic',
6     qos=0,
7     payload='some payload'.encode()
8 )
```

This allows you to test your Lambda functions in the cloud and migrate them to AWS Greengrass with minimal effort.

Note

The AWS SDK is natively part of the environment when executing a Lambda function in the AWS cloud. If you want to use `boto3` in a Lambda function deployed on an AWS Greengrass core, make sure to include the AWS SDK in your package. In addition, if you choose to use both the AWS Greengrass Core SDK and the AWS SDK simultaneously in the same package, your Lambda functions must use the correct namespace. For more information about how to create your deployment package, see:

AWS Lambda Creating a Deployment Package (Python) AWS Lambda Creating a Deployment Package (NodeJS) AWS Lambda Creating a Deployment Package (Java)

[GGC v1.0.0]

AWS SDKs

Using the AWS SDKs, you can build applications that work with any AWS service, including Amazon S3, Amazon DynamoDB, AWS IoT, AWS Greengrass, and more. In the context of AWS Greengrass, you can use the AWS SDK inside deployed Lambda functions to make direct calls to any AWS service.

AWS IoT Device SDKs

The AWS IoT Device SDKs helps devices connect to AWS IoT or AWS Greengrass services. Devices must know which AWS Greengrass group they belong to and the IP address of the AWS Greengrass core that they should connect to.

Although you can use any of the AWS IoT Device SDKs to connect to an AWS Greengrass core, only the C++ and Python Device SDKs provide AWS Greengrass-specific functionality, such as access to the AWS Greengrass Discovery Service and AWS Greengrass core root CA downloads. For more information, see AWS IoT Device SDK.

AWS Greengrass Core SDK

The AWS Greengrass Core SDK enables Lambda functions to interact with the AWS Greengrass core on which they run in order to publish messages, interact with the local Device Shadow service, or invoke other deployed Lambda functions. This SDK is used exclusively for writing Lambda functions running in the Lambda runtime on an AWS Greengrass core. Lambda functions running on an AWS Greengrass core can interact with AWS cloud services directly using the AWS SDK. The AWS Greengrass Core SDK and the AWS SDK are contained in different packages, so you can use both packages simultaneously. You can download the AWS Greengrass Core SDK from the **Software** page of the AWS IoT console.

The AWS Greengrass Core SDK follows the AWS SDK programming model. It allows you to easily port Lambda functions developed for the cloud to Lambda functions that run on an AWS Greengrass core. For example, using the AWS SDK, the following Lambda function publishes a message to the topic `"/some/topic"` in the cloud:

```
1 import boto3
2
3 client = boto3.client('iot-data')
4 response = client.publish(
5     topic = "/some/topic",
6     qos = 0,
7     payload = "Some payload".encode()
8 )
```

To port this Lambda function for execution on an AWS Greengrass core, replace the `import boto3` statement with the `import greengrasssdk`, as shown in the following snippet:

The AWS Greengrass Core SDK only supports sending MQTT messages with QoS = 0.

```
1 import greengrasssdk
2
3 client = greengrasssdk.client('iot-data')
4 response = client.publish(
5     topic='/some/topic',
```

```
6    qos=0,
7    payload='some payload'.encode()
8 )
```

This allows you to test your Lambda functions in the cloud and migrate them to AWS Greengrass with minimal effort.

Note
The AWS SDK is natively part of the environment when executing a Lambda function in the AWS cloud. If you want to use boto3 in a Lambda function deployed on an AWS Greengrass core, make sure to include the AWS SDK in your package. In addition, if you choose to use both the AWS Greengrass Core SDK and the AWS SDK simultaneously in the same package, your Lambda functions must use the correct namespace. For more information about how to create your deployment package, see:
AWS Lambda Creating a Deployment Package (Python)

Supported Platforms and Requirements

The AWS Greengrass core software is supported on the platforms listed below, and requires a few dependencies.

[GGC v1.5.0]
- Supported platforms:
  - Architecture: ARMv7l; OS: Linux; Distribution: Raspbian Jessie, 2017-03-02
  - Architecture: x86_64; OS: Linux; Distribution: Amazon Linux (amzn-ami-hvm-2016.09.1.20170119-x86_64-ebs)
  - Architecture: x86_64; OS: Linux; Distribution: Ubuntu 14.04 – 16.04
  - Architecture: ARMv8 (AArch64); OS: Linux; Distribution: Ubuntu 14.04 – 16.04 (Annapurna Alpine V2)
- The following items are required:
  - Minimum 128 MB RAM allocated to the AWS Greengrass core device.
  - Linux kernel version 4.4 or greater: while several versions may work with AWS Greengrass, for optimal security and performance, we recommend version 4.4 or greater.
  - Glibc library version 2.14 or greater.
  - The /var/run directory must be present on the device.
  - AWS Greengrass requires hardlink and softlink protection to be enabled on the device. Without this, AWS Greengrass can only be run in insecure mode, using the -i flag.
  - The ggc_user and ggc_group user and group must be present on the device.
  - The following Linux kernel configurations must be enabled on the device:
    - Namespace: CONFIG_IPC_NS, CONFIG_UTS_NS, CONFIG_USER_NS, CONFIG_PID_NS
    - CGroups: CONFIG_CGROUP_DEVICE, CONFIG_CGROUPS, CONFIG_MEMCG
    - Others: CONFIG_POSIX_MQUEUE, CONFIG_OVERLAY_FS, CONFIG_HAVE_ARCH_SECCOMP_FILTER, CONFIG_SECCOMP_FILTER, CONFIG_KEYS, CONFIG_SECCOMP
  - /dev/stdin, /dev/stdout, and /dev/stderr must be enabled.
  - The Linux kernel must support cgroups.
  - The *memory* cgroup must be enabled and mounted to allow AWS Greengrass to set the memory limit for Lambda functions.
  - The root certificate for Amazon S3 and AWS IoT must be present in the system trust store.
- The following items may be optional:

- The *devices* `cgroup` must be enabled and mounted if Lambda functions with Local Resource Access (LRA) are used to open files on the AWS Greengrass core device.
- Python version 2.7 is required if Python Lambda functions are used. If so, ensure that it's added to your `PATH` environment variable.
- NodeJS version 6.10 or greater is required if Node.JS Lambda functions are used. If so, ensure that it's added to your `PATH` environment variable.
- Java version 8 or greater is required if Java Lambda functions are used. If so, ensure that it's added to your `PATH` environment variable.
- OpenSSL 1.01 or greater is required for Greengrass OTA Agent as well as the following commands: `wget`, `realpath`, `tar`, `readlink`, `basename`, `dirname`, `pidof`, `df`, `grep`, and `umount`.

[GGC v1.3.0]

- Supported platforms:
  - Architecture: ARMv7l; OS: Linux; Distribution: Raspbian Jessie, 2017-03-02
  - Architecture: x86_64; OS: Linux; Distribution: Amazon Linux (amzn-ami-hvm-2016.09.1.20170119-x86_64-ebs)
  - Architecture: x86_64; OS: Linux; Distribution: Ubuntu 14.04 – 16.04
  - Architecture: ARMv8 (AArch64); OS: Linux; Distribution: Ubuntu 14.04 – 16.04 (Annapurna Alpine V2)
- The following items are required:
  - Minimum 128 MB RAM allocated to the AWS Greengrass core device.
  - Linux kernel version 4.4 or greater: while several versions may work with AWS Greengrass, for optimal security and performance, we recommend version 4.4 or greater.
  - Glibc library version 2.14 or greater.
  - The `/var/run` directory must be present on the device.
  - AWS Greengrass requires hardlink and softlink protection to be enabled on the device. Without this, AWS Greengrass can only be run in insecure mode, using the `-i` flag.
  - The `ggc_user` and `ggc_group` user and group must be present on the device.
  - The following Linux kernel configurations must be enabled on the device:
    - Namespace: CONFIG_IPC_NS, CONFIG_UTS_NS, CONFIG_USER_NS, CONFIG_PID_NS
    - CGroups: CONFIG_CGROUP_DEVICE, CONFIG_CGROUPS, CONFIG_MEMCG
    - Others: CONFIG_POSIX_MQUEUE, CONFIG_OVERLAY_FS, CONFIG_HAVE_ARCH_SECCOMP_FILTER, CONFIG_SECCOMP_FILTER, CONFIG_KEYS, CONFIG_SECCOMP
  - The https://www.sqlite.org/ package is required for AWS IoT device shadows. Ensure it's added to your `PATH` environment variable.
  - `/dev/stdin`, `/dev/stdout`, and `/dev/stderr` must be enabled.
  - The Linux kernel must support cgroups.
  - The *memory* `cgroup` must be enabled and mounted to allow AWS Greengrass to set the memory limit for Lambdas.
  - The root certificate for Amazon S3 and AWS IoT must be present in the system trust store.
- The following items may be optional:
  - The *devices* `cgroup` must be enabled and mounted if Lambdas with Local Resource Access (LRA) are used to open files on the AWS Greengrass core device.
  - Python version 2.7 is required if Python Lambdas are used. If so, ensure that it's added to your `PATH` environment variable.
  - NodeJS version 6.10 or greater is required if Node.JS Lambdas are used. If so, ensure that it's added to your `PATH` environment variable.
  - Java version 8 or greater is required if Java Lambdas are used. If so, ensure that it's added to your `PATH` environment variable.

- OpenSSL 1.01 or greater is required for Greengrass OTA Agent as well as the following commands: `wget`, `realpath`, `tar`, `readlink`, `basename`, `dirname`, `pidof`, `df`, `grep`, and `umount`.

[GGC v1.1.0]

- Supported platforms:
  - Architecture: ARMv7l; OS: Linux; Distribution: Raspbian Jessie, 2017-03-02
  - Architecture: x86_64; OS: Linux; Distribution: Amazon Linux (amzn-ami-hvm-2016.09.1.20170119-x86_64-ebs)
  - Architecture: x86_64; OS: Linux; Distribution: Ubuntu 14.04 – 16.04
  - Architecture: ARMv8 (AArch64); OS: Linux; Distribution: Ubuntu 14.04 – 16.04 (Annapurna Alpine V2)
- The following items are required:
  - Minimum 128 MB RAM allocated to the AWS Greengrass core device.
  - Linux kernel version 4.4 or greater: while several versions may work with AWS Greengrass, for optimal security and performance, we recommend version 4.4 or greater.
  - Glibc library version 2.14 or greater.
  - The `/var/run` directory must be present on the device.
  - AWS Greengrass requires hardlink and softlink protection to be enabled on the device. Without this, AWS Greengrass can only be run in insecure mode, using the `-i` flag.
  - The `ggc_user` and `ggc_group` user and group must be present on the device.
  - The following Linux kernel configurations must be enabled on the device:
    - Namespace: CONFIG_IPC_NS, CONFIG_UTS_NS, CONFIG_USER_NS, CONFIG_PID_NS
    - CGroups: CONFIG_CGROUP_DEVICE, CONFIG_CGROUPS, CONFIG_MEMCG
    - Others: CONFIG_POSIX_MQUEUE, CONFIG_OVERLAY_FS, CONFIG_HAVE_ARCH_SECCOMP_FILTER, CONFIG_SECCOMP_FILTER, CONFIG_KEYS, CONFIG_SECCOMP
  - The https://www.sqlite.org/ package is required for AWS IoT device shadows. Ensure it's added to your `PATH` environment variable.
  - `/dev/stdin`, `/dev/stdout`, and `/dev/stderr` must be enabled.
  - The Linux kernel must support cgroups.
  - The *memory* `cgroup` must be enabled and mounted to allow AWS Greengrass to set the memory limit for Lambdas.
  - The root certificate for Amazon S3 and AWS IoT must be present in the system trust store.
- The following items may be optional:
  - Python version 2.7 is required if Python Lambdas are used. If so, ensure that it's added to your `PATH` environment variable.
  - NodeJS version 6.10 or greater is required if Node.JS Lambdas are used. If so, ensure that it's added to your `PATH` environment variable.
  - Java version 8 or greater is required if Java Lambdas are used. If so, ensure that it's added to your `PATH` environment variable.

[GGC v1.0.0]

- Supported platforms:
  - Architecture: ARMv7l; OS: Linux; Distribution: Raspbian Jessie, 2017-03-02
  - Architecture: x86_64; OS: Linux; Distribution: Amazon Linux (amzn-ami-hvm-2016.09.1.20170119-x86_64-ebs)
  - Architecture: x86_64; OS: Linux; Distribution: Ubuntu 14.04 – 16.04

- Architecture: ARMv8 (AArch64); OS: Linux; Distribution: Ubuntu 14.04 – 16.04 (Annapurna Alpine V2)
- The following items are required:
  - Minimum 128 MB RAM allocated to the AWS Greengrass core device.
  - Linux kernel version 4.4 or greater: while several versions may work with AWS Greengrass, for optimal security and performance, we recommend version 4.4 or greater.
  - Glibc library version 2.14 or greater.
  - The /var/run directory must be present on the device.
  - AWS Greengrass requires hardlink and softlink protection to be enabled on the device. Without this, AWS Greengrass can only be run in insecure mode, using the -i flag.
  - The ggc_user and ggc_group user and group must be present on the device.
  - The following Linux kernel configurations must be enabled on the device:
    - Namespace: CONFIG_IPC_NS, CONFIG_UTS_NS, CONFIG_USER_NS, CONFIG_PID_NS
    - CGroups: CONFIG_CGROUP_DEVICE, CONFIG_CGROUPS, CONFIG_MEMCG
    - Others: CONFIG_POSIX_MQUEUE, CONFIG_OVERLAY_FS, CONFIG_HAVE_ARCH_SECCOMP_FILTER, CONFIG_SECCOMP_FILTER, CONFIG_KEYS, CONFIG_SECCOMP
  - The https://www.sqlite.org/ package is required for AWS IoT device shadows. Ensure it's added to your PATH environment variable.
  - /dev/stdin, /dev/stdout, and /dev/stderr must be enabled.
  - The Linux kernel must support cgroups.
  - The *memory* cgroup must be enabled and mounted to allow AWS Greengrass to set the memory limit for Lambdas.
  - The root certificate for Amazon S3 and AWS IoT must be present in the system trust store.
- The following items may be optional:
  - Python version 2.7 is required if Python Lambdas are used. If so, ensure that it's added to your PATH environment variable.

Getting Started with AWS Greengrass

This tutorial includes six modules, each designed to show you AWS Greengrass basics and help you get started in as few steps as possible. This tutorial covers:

- The AWS Greengrass programming model.
- Fundamental concepts, such as AWS Greengrass cores, groups, and subscriptions.
- The deployment process for running AWS Lambda functions at the edge.

Requirements

To complete this tutorial, you will need the following:

- A Mac, Windows PC, or UNIX-like system.

- An Amazon Web Services (AWS) account. If you don't have an AWS account, see Create an AWS Account.

- The use of an AWS region that supports AWS Greengrass such as US East (N. Virginia), US West (Oregon), EU (Frankfurt), Asia Pacific (Sydney), Asia Pacific (Tokyo) – for more information, see AWS Greengrass FAQs. **Important**
  Make note of your region to ensure that it is consistently used throughout this tutorial – inadvertently switching regions midway through the tutorial would be problematic. Note that the last exercise in this tutorial assumes the US East (N. Virgina) region, so you may want to only use the US East (N. Virgina) region, as possible.

- A Raspberry Pi 3 Model B with a 8 GB microSD card, or an Amazon EC2 instance. Because AWS Greengrass is intended to be used with physical hardware, we recommend that you use a Raspberry Pi. **Note**
  If the model of your Raspberry Pi is unknown, you can run the following command:

```
1 cat /proc/cpuinfo
```

Near the bottom of the listing, note the value of the `Revision` attribute. You can determine the model of your Pi by using this value along with the table at Which Pi have I got? For example, if the value of `Revision` is `a02082`, then from the table we see that the Pi is a 3 Model B. Additionally, the architecture of your Pi must be `armv71` or greater. To determine the architecture of your Raspberry Pi, run the following command:

```
1 uname -m
```

The result must be greater than or equal to `armv71`.

- Basic familiarity with Python 2.7.

Although this tutorial focuses on running AWS Greengrass on a Raspberry Pi or an Amazon EC2 instance, other platforms are supported. For more information, see Supported Platforms and Requirements.

Create an AWS Account

If you don't have an AWS account, follow these steps:

1. Open the AWS home page, and choose **Create an AWS Account**. **Note**
   If you've signed in to AWS recently, you might see **Sign In to the Console** instead.

2. Follow the online instructions. Part of the sign-up procedure involves receiving a phone call and entering a PIN using your phone keypad. **Important**
   Ensure that your account has administrative privileges before proceeding.

Module 1: Environment Setup for Greengrass

This module shows you how to get an out-of-the-box Raspberry Pi, Amazon EC2 instance, or other device ready to be used by AWS Greengrass.

Important
Use the **Filter View** drop-down list in the upper-right corner of this webpage to choose your platform.

This module should take less than 30 minutes to complete.

Setting Up a Raspberry Pi

If you are setting up a Raspberry Pi for the first time, you must follow all of these steps. If you are using an existing Raspberry Pi, you can skip to step 9. However, we recommend that you re-image your Raspberry Pi with the operating system as recommended in step 2.

1. Download and install an SD card formatter such as SD Memory Card Formatter or PiBakery. Insert the SD card into your computer. Start the program and choose the drive where your have inserted your SD card. You can quick format the SD card.

2. Download the Raspbian Jessie operating system as a `.zip` file. Only `2017-03-02-raspbian-jessie.zip` is currently supported by AWS Greengrass.

3. Using an SD card-writing tool (such as Etcher), follow the tool's instructions to flash the downloaded `2017-03-02-raspbian-jessie.zip` file onto the SD card. Because the operating system image is large, this step might take some time. Eject your SD card from your computer, and insert the microSD card into your Raspberry Pi.

4. For the first boot, we recommend that you connect the Raspberry Pi to a monitor (through HDMI), a keyboard, and a mouse. Next, connect your Pi to a micro USB power source and the Raspbian operating system should start up.

5. You may want to configure the Pi's keyboard layout before proceeding. To do so, choose the Raspberry icon in the upper-right, choose **Preferences** and then **Mouse and Keyboard Settings**. Next, choose the **Keyboard** tab, **Keyboard Layout**, and then choose an appropriate keyboard variant.

6. Next, connect your Raspberry Pi to the internet through a Wi-Fi network or an Ethernet cable. **Note** Connect your Raspberry Pi to the *same* network that your computer is connected to, and be sure that both your computer and Raspberry Pi have internet access before proceeding. If you're in a work environment or behind a firewall, you may need to connect your Pi and your computer to the guest network in order to get both devices on the same network. This approach, however, may disconnect your computer from local network resources such as your intranet. One solution may be to connect the Pi to the guest Wi-Fi network, your computer to the guest Wi-Fi network *and* your local network through an Ethernet cable. In this configuration, your computer should be able to connect to the Raspberry Pi via the guest Wi-Fi network and your local network resources through the Ethernet cable.

7. You must set up SSH on your Pi to remotely connect to it. On your Raspberry Pi, open a terminal window and run the following command:

```
1 sudo raspi-config
```

   You should see the following:

```
┌──────┤ Raspberry Pi Software Configuration Tool (raspi-config) ├──────┐
│                                                                        │
│    1 Change User Password        Change password for the default u     │
│    2 Hostname                     Set the visible name for this Pi      │
│    3 Boot Options                 Configure options for start-up        │
│    4 Localisation Options         Set up language and regional sett     │
│    5 Interfacing Options          Configure connections to peripher     │
│    6 Overclock                    Configure overclocking for your P     │
│    7 Advanced Options             Configure advanced settings           │
│    8 Update                       Update this tool to the latest ve     │
│    9 About raspi-config           Information about this configurat     │
│                                                                        │
│                                                                        │
│                  <Select>                       <Finish>               │
│                                                                        │
└────────────────────────────────────────────────────────────────────────┘
```

Scroll down and choose **Interfacing Options** and then choose **P2 SSH**. When prompted, choose **Yes** using the Tab key (followed by Enter). SSH should now be enabled, choose **OK**. Tab key to **Finish** and then press the Enter key. Lastly, reboot your Pi by running the following command:

```
1  sudo reboot
```

8. On your Raspberry Pi, run the following command in the terminal:

```
1  hostname -I
```

This returns the IP address of your Raspberry Pi. **Note**
For the following, if you receive an ECDSA key fingerprint related message `Are you sure you want to continue connecting (yes/no)?`, enter `yes`. Additionally, the default password for the Raspberry Pi is **raspberry**.

If you are using macOS, open a Terminal window and type the following:

```
1  ssh pi@IP-address
```

Here, *IP-address* corresponds to the IP address of your Raspberry Pi that you obtained by using the prior `hostname -I` command.

If you are using Windows, you need to install and configure PuTTY. Choose **Connection**, **Data**, and make sure that **Prompt** is selected:

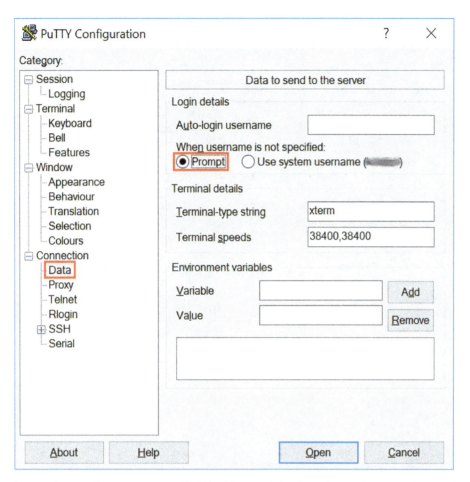

Next, choose **Session**, type the IP address of the Raspberry Pi, and choose **Open** using default settings. For example (your IP address, in all likelihood, will be different):

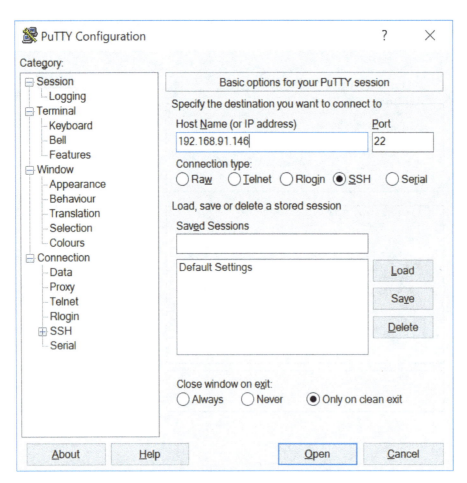

If a PuTTY Security Alert dialog is displayed, choose an appropriate response such as **Yes**.

This will result in a terminal window similar to the following. The default Raspberry Pi login and password are **pi** and **raspberry**, respectively.

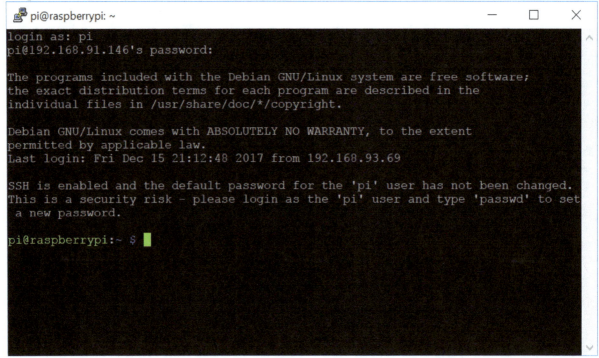

Note

If your computer is connected to a remote network using VPN (such as a work related network), this may cause difficulty connecting from the computer to the Raspberry Pi using SSH.

9. You are now ready to set up the Raspberry Pi for AWS Greengrass. First, run the following commands from a local Raspberry Pi terminal window or an SSH terminal window:

```
1 sudo adduser --system ggc_user
2 sudo addgroup --system ggc_group
```

10. Run the following commands to update the Linux kernel version of your Raspberry Pi.

```
1 sudo apt-get install rpi-update
2 sudo rpi-update b81a11258fc911170b40a0b09bbd63c84bc5ad59
```

Although several kernel versions might work with AWS Greengrass, for the best security and performance, we recommend that you use the kernel version indicated in step 2. In order to activate the new firmware, reboot your Raspberry Pi:

```
1 sudo reboot
```

As applicable, reconnect to the Raspberry Pi using SSH after minute or so. Next, run the following command to ensure you have the correct kernel version:

```
1 uname -a
```

You should receive output similar to the following, the key item being the Linux Raspberry Pi version information 4.9.30:

```
[pi@raspberrypi:~ $ uname -a
Linux raspberrypi 4.9.30-v7+ #1001 SMP Fri May 26 16:09:18 BST 2017 armv7l GNU/Linux
```

11. To improve security on the Pi device, run the following commands to enable hardlink and softlink protection at operating system start-up.

```
1 cd /etc/sysctl.d
2 ls
```

If you see the 98-rpi.conf file, use a text editor (such as leafpad, nano, or vi) to add the following two lines to the end of the file (you can run the text editor using the sudo command to avoid write permission issues, as in sudo nano 98-rpi.conf).

```
1 fs.protected_hardlinks = 1
2 fs.protected_symlinks = 1
```

If you do not see the 98-rpi.conf file, follow the instructions in the README.sysctl file.

Now reboot the Pi:

```
1 sudo reboot
```

After about a minute, connect to the Pi using SSH as applicable and then run the following commands from a Raspberry Pi terminal to confirm the hardlink/symlink change:

```
1 sudo sysctl -a 2> /dev/null | grep fs.protected
```

You should see fs.protected_hardlinks = 1 and fs.protected_symlinks = 1.

12. Your Raspberry Pi should now be ready for AWS Greengrass. To ensure that you have all of the dependencies required for AWS Greengrass, download the AWS Greengrass dependency checker .zip file from the GitHub repository and run it on the Pi as follows:

```
1 cd /home/pi/Downloads
2 git clone https://github.com/aws-samples/aws-greengrass-samples.git
3 cd aws-greengrass-samples
4 cd greengrass-dependency-checker-GGCv1.5.0
5 sudo modprobe configs
6 sudo ./check_ggc_dependencies | more
```

With respect to the `more` command, press the Spacebar key to display another screen of text. **Important** Because this tutorial only uses the AWS IoT Device SDK for Python, you can ignore warnings about the missing optional NodeJS 6.10 and Java 8 prerequisites that the `check_ggc_dependencies` script may produce.

For information about the `modprobe` command, you can run `man modprobe` in the terminal.

Your Raspberry Pi configuration is complete. Continue to Module 2: Installing the Greengrass Core Software.

Setting Up an Amazon EC2 Instance

1. Sign in to the AWS Management Console and launch an Amazon EC2 instance using an Amazon Linux AMI (Amazon Machine Image). For information about Amazon EC2 instances, see the Amazon EC2 Getting Started Guide.

2. After your Amazon EC2 instance is running, enable port 8883 to allow incoming MQTT communications so that other devices can connect with the AWS Greengrass core. In the left pane of the Amazon EC2 console, choose **Security Groups**.

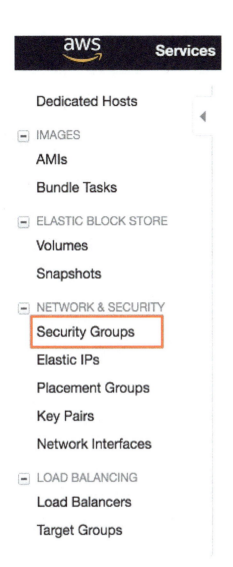

Choose the instance that you just launched, and then choose the **Inbound** tab.

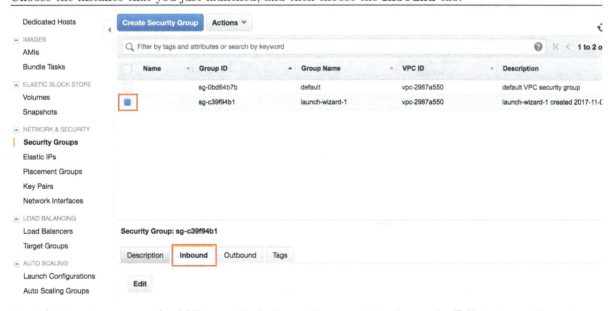

By default, only one port for SSH is enabled. To enable port 8883, choose the **Edit** button. Next, choose the **Add Rule** button and create a custom TCP rule as shown below, then choose **Save**.

3. In the left pane, choose **Instances**, choose your instance, and then choose the **Connect** button. Connect to your Amazon EC2 instance by using SSH. You can use PuTTY for Windows or Terminal for macOS.

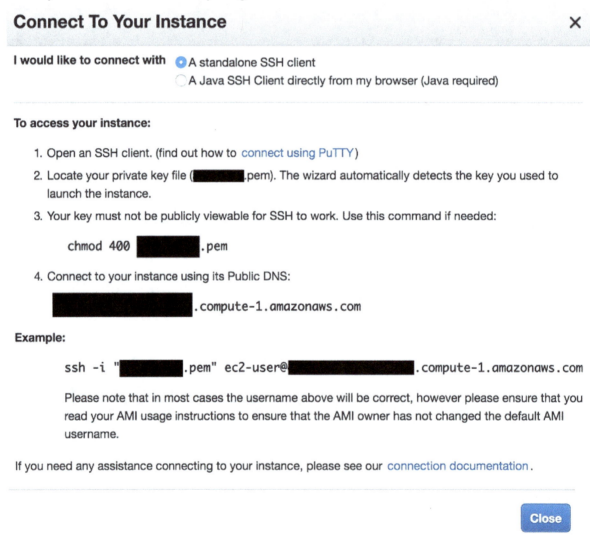

4. Once connected to your Amazon EC2 instance through SSH, run the following commands to create user `ggc_user` and group `ggc_group`:

```
1 sudo adduser --system ggc_user
2 sudo groupadd --system ggc_group
```

5. To improve security on the device, enable hardlink/softlink protection on the operating system at start-up. To do so, run the following commands:

```
1 cd /etc/sysctl.d
2 ls
```

Using your favorite text editor (`leadpad`, `nano`, `vi`, etc.), add the following two lines to the end of the `00-defaults.conf` file, You might need to change permissions (using the `chmod` command) to write to the file, or use the `sudo` command to edit as root (for example, `sudo nano 00-defaults.conf`).

```
1 fs.protected_hardlinks = 1
2 fs.protected_symlinks = 1
```

Run the following command to reboot the Amazon EC2 instance.

```
1 sudo reboot
```

After a few minutes, connect to your instance by using SSH as above. Then, run the following command to confirm the change.

```
1 sudo sysctl -a | grep fs.protected
```

You should see that hardlinks and softlinks are set to 1.

6. Extract and run the following script to mount Linux control groups (**cgroups**). This is an AWS Greengrass dependency:

```
1 curl https://raw.githubusercontent.com/tianon/cgroupfs-mount/951
    c38ee8d802330454bdede20d85ec1c0f8d312/cgroupfs-mount > cgroupfs-mount.sh
2 chmod +x cgroupfs-mount.sh
3 sudo bash ./cgroupfs-mount.sh
```

Your Amazon EC2 instance should now be ready for AWS Greengrass. To be sure that you have all of the dependencies, extract and run the following AWS Greengrass dependency script from the GitHub repository:

```
1 sudo yum install git
2 git clone https://github.com/aws-samples/aws-greengrass-samples.git
3 cd aws-greengrass-samples
4 cd greengrass-dependency-checker-GGCv1.5.0
5 sudo ./check_ggc_dependencies
```

Your Amazon EC2 instance configuration is complete. Continue to Module 2: Installing the Greengrass Core Software.

Setting Up Other Devices

If you are new to AWS Greengrass, we recommend that you use a Raspberry Pi or an Amazon EC2 instance and follow the steps provided above to set up the device. Follow the below steps to make your own AWS Greengrass-supported device ready for AWS Greengrass.

1. To make sure you have other devices ready to run AWS Greengrass, download and extract the Greengrass dependency checker from the GitHub repository, and then run the following commands:

```
1 git clone https://github.com/aws-samples/aws-greengrass-samples.git
2 cd greengrass-dependency-checker-GGCv1.5.0
3 sudo ./check_ggc_dependencies
```

This script runs on AWS Greengrass supported platforms and requires the following Linux system commands:

```
1 printf, uname, cat, ls, head, find, zcat, awk, sed, sysctl, wc, cut, sort, expr, grep, test
    , dirname, readlink, xargs, strings, uniq
```

2. Install all required dependencies on your device, as indicated by the dependency script. For missing kernel-level dependencies, you might have to recompile your kernel. For mounting Linux control groups (`cgroups`), you can run the cgroupfs-mount script. **Note**
   If no errors appear in the output, AWS Greengrass should be able to run successfully on your device.

   For the list of AWS Greengrass requirements and dependencies, see Supported Platforms and Requirements.

Configuring NVIDIA Jetson TX2 for AWS Greengrass

If your core device is an NVIDIA Jetson TX2, it must be configured before you can install the AWS Greengrass. The following steps describe how to flash the firmware to a JetPack installer and rebuild the kernel so that the device is ready to install the AWS Greengrass core software.

Note
The JetPack installer version that you use is based on your target CUDA Toolkit version. The following instructions assume that you're using JetPack 3.1 and CUDA Toolkit 8.0, because the binaries for TensorFlow v1.4.0 that AWS Greengrass provides for machine learning (ML) inference are compiled against this version of CUDA. For more information about AWS Greengrass ML inference, see Perform Machine Learning Inference.

Flash the JetPack 3.1 Firmware

1. On a physical desktop that is running Ubuntu 14 or 16, flash the firmware to JetPack 3.1, as described in Download and Install JetPack L4T.

   Follow the instructions in the installer to install all the packages and dependencies on the Jetson board, which must be connected to the desktop with a Micro-B cable. Start the device in forced recovery mode.
   Note
   After the JetPack installation, you must use *ubuntu* credentials to log onto the device. The SSH agent hangs when it tries to log in using any other account, even if you SSH directly to the board using this account.

2. Reboot your board in normal mode, and then connect a display to the board.

Rebuild the NVIDIA Jetson TX2 Kernel

Run the following commands on the Jetson board.

1. Check the kernel configurations:

```
1 nvidia@tegra-ubuntu:~$ zcat /proc/config.gz | grep -e CONFIG_KEYS -e CONFIG_POSIX_MQUEUE -e
    CONFIG_OF_OVERLAY -e CONFIG_OVERLAY_FS -e CONFIG_HAVE_ARCH_SECCOMP_FILTER -e
    CONFIG_SECCOMP_FILTER -e CONFIG_SECCOMP -e CONFIG_DEVPTS_MULTIPLE_INSTANCES -e
    CONFIG_IPC_NS -e CONFIG_NET_NS -e CONFIG_UTS_NS -e CONFIG_USER_NS -e CONFIG_PID_NS -e
    CONFIG_CGROUPS -e CONFIG_MEMCG -e CONFIG_CGROUP_FREEZER -e CONFIG_CGROUP_DEVICE
2 # CONFIG_POSIX_MQUEUE is not set
3 CONFIG_CGROUPS=y
4 CONFIG_CGROUP_FREEZER=y
5 # CONFIG_CGROUP_DEVICE is not set
6 # CONFIG_MEMCG is not set
7 CONFIG_UTS_NS=y
8 CONFIG_IPC_NS=y
9 # CONFIG_USER_NS is not set
10 CONFIG_PID_NS=y
11 CONFIG_NET_NS=y
```

```
12 CONFIG_HAVE_ARCH_SECCOMP_FILTER=y
13 CONFIG_SECCOMP_FILTER=y
14 CONFIG_SECCOMP=y
15 # CONFIG_OF_OVERLAY is not set
16 CONFIG_DEVPTS_MULTIPLE_INSTANCES=y
17 # CONFIG_OVERLAY_FS is not set
18 # CONFIG_KEYS is not set
```

2. Check the performance and power settings:

```
1 nvidia@tegra-ubuntu:~$ sudo nvpmodel -q
2 NV Power Mode: MAXP_CORE_ARM
3 3
```

3. Put the Jetson into high performance mode:

```
1 nvidia@tegra-ubuntu:~$ sudo nvpmodel -m 0
```

4. Clone the git repository:

```
1 nvidia@tegra-ubuntu:~$ cd /
2 nvidia@tegra-ubuntu:~$ sudo git clone https://github.com/jetsonhacks/buildJetsonTX2Kernel.
      git
```

5. Modify the `getKernelSources.sh` script, based on the following diff of the changes:

```
1 index f47f28d..3dd863a 100755
2 --- a/scripts/getKernelSources.sh
3 +++ b/scripts/getKernelSources.sh
4 @@ -1,12 +1,15 @@
5 #!/bin/bash
6 apt-add-repository universe
7 apt-get update
8 -apt-get install qt5-default pkg-config -y
9 +apt-get install qt5-default pkg-config libncurses5-dev libssl-dev -y
10 cd /usr/src
11 wget http://developer.download.nvidia.com/embedded/L4T/r28_Release_v1.0/BSP/source_release
      .tbz2
12 tar -xvf source_release.tbz2 sources/kernel_src-tx2.tbz2
13 tar -xvf sources/kernel_src-tx2.tbz2
14 cd kernel/kernel-4.4
15 +make clean
16 zcat /proc/config.gz > .config
17 -make xconfig
18 +echo "type something to continue"
19 +read
20 +make menuconfig
```

6. Run the getKernelSources script:

```
1 nvidia@tegra-ubuntu:~$ cd /buildJetsonTX2Kernel
2 nvidia@tegra-ubuntu:~$ sudo ./getKernelSources.sh
```

7. When prompted for "type something to continue", press **CTRL + Z** to background the script.

8. Go to /usr/src/kernel/kernel-4.4/security/keys and edit the `Kconfig` file by adding the following lines between `KEYS` and `PERSISTENT_KEYRINGS`:

```
1 config KEYS_COMPAT
2     def_bool y
3     depends on COMPAT && KEYS
```

9. Unpause the script:

```
1 nvidia@tegra-ubuntu:~$ cd /usr/src/kernel/kernel-4.4/
2 nvidia@tegra-ubuntu:~$ fg
```

Type some characters to unblock the script.

10. In the setup window that opens, choose **Enable loadable module support**, and then open the submenu to enable **optionModule** signature verification. Use the arrow keys to move and the spacebar to select any option. Then, save the change and exit.

11. Verify that KEYS_COMPAT is enabled:

```
1 nvidia@tegra-ubuntu:~$ grep --color KEYS_COMPAT /usr/src/kernel/kernel-4.4/.config
```

12. Open the kernel configuration interface and enable kernel configurations:

```
1 nvidia@tegra-ubuntu:~$ sudo make xconfig
```

A window opens that shows all the kernel configurations. Use **FIND** to search for the following keywords and tick-mark them. **Note**
Keywords vary by configuration. The following list contains alternative versions in parentheses that can help you find the equivalent keywords for your configuration.

- CONFIG_POSIX_MQUEUE (POSIX Message Queue)
- CONFIG_OF_OVERLAY (Overlay Filesystem Support)
- CONFIG_OVERLAY_FS (Overlay Filesystem Support)
- CONFIG_USER_NS (User Namespace)
- CONFIG_MEMCG (Memory Resource Controller for Control Group)
- CONFIG_CGROUP_DEVICE (Device Controller for cgroups)

13. Build the kernel:

```
1 nvidia@tegra-ubuntu:~$ cd /buildJetsonTX2Kernel
2 nvidia@tegra-ubuntu:~$ sudo ./makeKernel.sh
```

14. Verify that the kernel configurations are enabled:

```
1 nvidia@tegra-ubuntu:~$ grep --color CONFIG_POSIX_MQUEUE /usr/src/kernel/kernel-4.4/.config
2 nvidia@tegra-ubuntu:~$ grep --color CONFIG_OF_OVERLAY /usr/src/kernel/kernel-4.4/.config
3 nvidia@tegra-ubuntu:~$ grep --color CONFIG_OVERLAY_FS /usr/src/kernel/kernel-4.4/.config
4 nvidia@tegra-ubuntu:~$ grep --color CONFIG_USER_NS /usr/src/kernel/kernel-4.4/.config
5 nvidia@tegra-ubuntu:~$ grep --color CONFIG_MEMCG /usr/src/kernel/kernel-4.4/.config
6 nvidia@tegra-ubuntu:~$ grep --color CONFIG_CGROUP_DEVICE /usr/src/kernel/kernel-4.4/.config
7 nvidia@tegra-ubuntu:~$ grep --color CONFIG_KEYS_COMPAT /usr/src/kernel/kernel-4.4/.config
8 nvidia@tegra-ubuntu:~$ grep --color CONFIG_COMPAT /usr/src/kernel/kernel-4.4/.config
9 nvidia@tegra-ubuntu:~$ grep --color CONFIG_KEYS /usr/src/kernel/kernel-4.4/.config
```

15. Copy the image:

```
1 nvidia@tegra-ubuntu:~$ sudo ./copyImage.sh
```

Module 2: Installing the Greengrass Core Software

This module shows you how to install the AWS Greengrass core software on your device. Before you begin, make sure that you have completed Module 1.

The AWS Greengrass core software provides the following functionality:

- Allows deployment and execution of local applications that are created by using AWS Lambda functions and managed through the deployment API.
- Enables local messaging between devices over a secure network by using a managed subscription scheme through the MQTT protocol.
- Ensures secure connections between devices and the cloud using device authentication and authorization.
- Provides secure, over-the-air, software updates of user-defined Lambda functions.

This module should take less than 30 minutes to complete.

Configure AWS Greengrass on AWS IoT

1. Sign in to the AWS Management Console on your computer and open the AWS IoT console. If this is the first time opening this console, choose **Get started**.

   Next, choose **Greengrass**:

   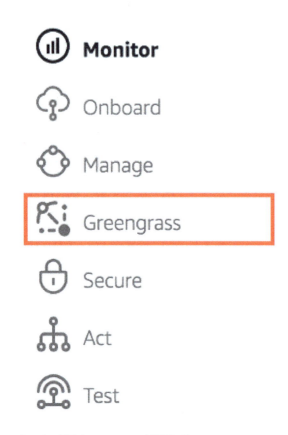

2. On the **Welcome to AWS Greengrass** page, choose **Get Started**:

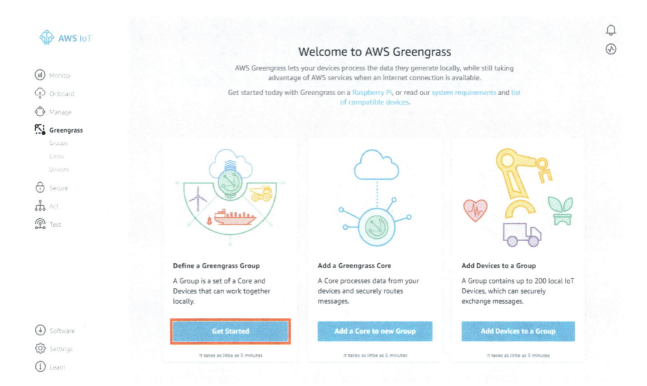

3. Create an AWS Greengrass group. An AWS Greengrass group contains information about the devices and how messages are processed in the group. Each AWS Greengrass group requires an AWS Greengrass core device that processes messages sent within the group. An AWS Greengrass core needs a certificate and an AWS IoT policy to access AWS Greengrass and AWS Cloud Services. On the **Set up your Greengrass group** page, choose **Use easy creation**.

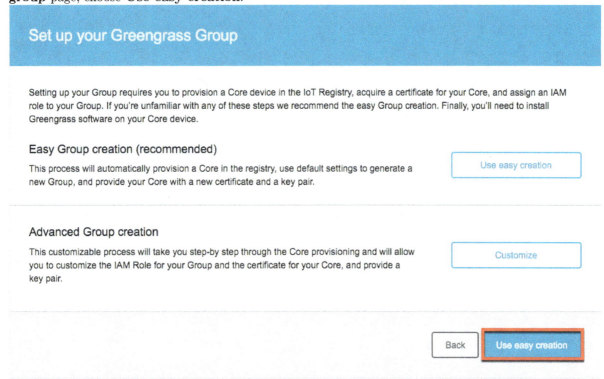

4. Type a name for your group (for example, **MyFirstGroup**), then choose **Next**:

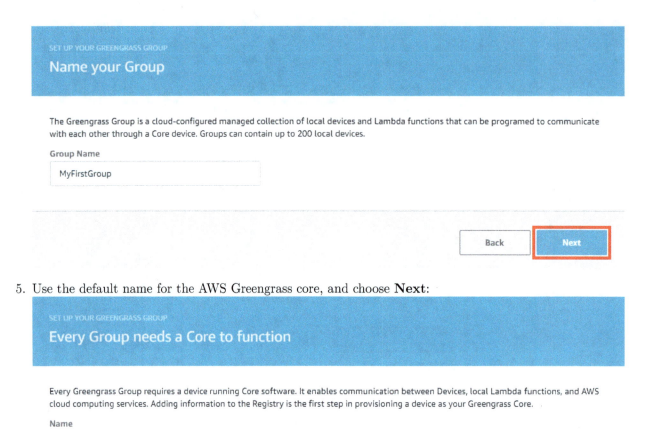

5. Use the default name for the AWS Greengrass core, and choose **Next**:

6. On the **Run a scripted easy Group creation** page, choose **Create Group and Core**.

Run a scripted easy Group creation

In order to speed up and simplify Group creation AWS Greengrass will handle the following processes and use default settings. By proceeding to the next step, you are giving permission for us to complete the following steps.

AWS Greengrass will take these actions on your behalf using default settings:

Create a new Greengrass Group in the cloud	Learn more
Provision a new Core in the IoT Registry and add to the Group	Learn more
Generate public and private key set for your Core	Learn more
Generate a new security certificate for the Core using the keys	Learn more
Attach a default security policy to the certificate	Learn more

Back   **Create Group and Core**

AWS IoT creates an AWS Greengrass group for you with default security policies and configuration files for you to load onto your device.

7. On the confirmation page, download your core's security resources and the AWS Greengrass Core software, as follows:

    1. Under **Download and store your Core's security resources**, choose **Download these resources as a tar.gz** to download the required security resources for your AWS Greengrass core.

Download and store your Core's security resources

A certificate for this Core	c6973960cc.cert.pem
A public key	c6973960cc.public.key
A private key	c6973960cc.private.key
Core-specific config file	config.json

Download these resources as a tar.gz

    2. Under **Download the current Greengrass Core software**, choose the CPU architecture (and operating system, if necessary) that best describes your core device:

- If you're using a Raspberry Pi, download the ARMv7l for Raspbian Jessie package.
- If you're using an Amazon EC2 instance, download one of the x86_64 packages.

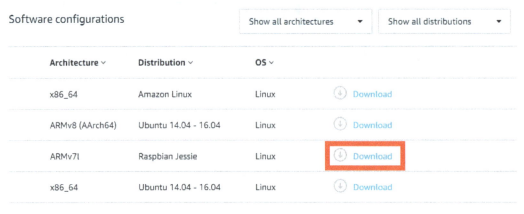

By downloading this software you agree to the Greengrass Core Software License Agreement .

> **Important**
> You must download both the security resources *and* the AWS Greengrass Core software before you choose **Finish**.

8. After downloading the security resources and the AWS Greengrass Core software, choose **Finish**.

   The group configuration page is displayed in the console:

GREENGRASS GROUP
MyFirstGroup
Not deployed

Actions ▾

Deployments
Subscriptions
Cores
Devices
Lambdas
Resources
Settings

Group history overview

By deployment ▾

There are no deployments for this Greengrass Group yet.

Start AWS Greengrass on the Core Device

1. In the prior step, you downloaded two files from the AWS Greengrass console:

   - `greengrass-OS-architecture-1.5.0.tar.gz` - this compressed file contains the AWS Greengrass core software that runs on the AWS Greengrass core device.
   - `GUID-setup.tar.gz` - this compressed file contains security certificates enabling secure communications with the AWS IoT cloud and `config.json` which contains configuration information specific to your AWS Greengrass core and the AWS IoT endpoint.

   If you don't recall the IP address of your AWS Greengrass core device, open a terminal on the AWS Greengrass core device and run the following command:

   ```
   1 hostname -I
   ```

   Based on your operating system, choose a tab to transfer the two compressed files from your computer to the AWS Greengrass core device: **Note**
   Recall that the default login and password for the Raspberry Pi is **pi** and **raspberry**, respectively.

[Windows]

To transfer the compressed files from your computer to a Raspberry Pi AWS Greengrass core device, use a convenient tool such as WinSCP or PuTTY's `pscp` command. To use the `pscp` command, open a Command Prompt window on your computer and run the following:

```
1 cd path-to-downloaded-files
2 pscp -pw Pi-password greengrass-OS-architecture-1.5.0.tar.gz pi@IP-address:/home/pi
3 pscp -pw Pi-password GUID-setup.tar.gz pi@IP-address:/home/pi
```

For example:

```
C:\>cd Users_____\Downloads

C:\Users_____\Downloads>pscp -pw raspberry 851a2ed30a-setup.tar.gz pi@10.0.0.12:/home/pi
851a2ed30a-setup.tar.gz   | 2 kB |   2.7 kB/s | ETA: 00:00:00 | 100%

C:\Users_____\Downloads>pscp -pw raspberry greengrass-linux-armv7l-1.3.0.tar.gz pi@10.0.0.12:/home/pi
greengrass-linux-armv7l-1 | 16820 kB | 480.6 kB/s | ETA: 00:00:00 | 100%
```

[macOS]

To transfer the compressed files from your Mac to a Raspberry Pi AWS Greengrass core device, open a Terminal window on your computer and run the following commands (note that *path-to-downloaded-files* is typically `~/Downloads`).

Note
You may be prompted for two passwords. If so, the first password is for the Mac's **sudo** command and the second will be the password for the Raspberry Pi.

```
1 cd path-to-downloaded-files
2 sudo scp greengrass-OS-architecture-1.5.0.tar.gz pi@IP-address:/home/pi
3 sudo scp GUID-setup.tar.gz pi@IP-address:/home/pi
```

[UNIX-like system]

To transfer the compressed files from your computer to a Raspberry Pi AWS Greengrass core device, open a terminal window on your computer and run the following commands:

```
1 cd path-to-downloaded-files
2 sudo scp greengrass-OS-architecture-1.5.0.tar.gz pi@IP-address:/home/pi
3 sudo scp GUID-setup.tar.gz pi@IP-address:/home/pi
```

[Raspberry Pi web browser]

If you used the Raspberry Pi's web browser to download the compressed files, the files should be in the Pi's ~/Downloads folder (i.e., /home/pi/Downloads). Otherwise, the compressed files should be in the Pi's ~ folder (i.e., /home/pi).

Open a terminal on the AWS Greengrass core device and navigate to the folder containing the compressed files (i.e., *path-to-compressed-files*).

```
1 cd path-to-compressed-files
```

Next, run the following commands to decompress the AWS Greengrass core binary file and the security resources (certificates, etc.) file:

```
1 sudo tar -xzvf greengrass-OS-architecture-1.5.0.tar.gz -C /
2 sudo tar -xzvf GUID-setup.tar.gz -C /greengrass
```

Among other things, the first command creates the /greengrass directory in the root folder of the AWS Greengrass core device (via the -C / argument). The second command copies the certificates into the /greengrass /certs folder and the config.json file into the /greengrass/config folder (via the -C /greengrass argument). For more information, see config.json Parameter Summary.

1. Install the Symantec VeriSign root CA onto your device. This certificate enables your device to communicate with AWS IoT using the MQTT messaging protocol over TLS. Make sure the AWS Greengrass core device is connected to the internet, then run the following commands (note that -O is the capital letter O):

   ```
   1 cd /greengrass/certs/
   2 sudo wget -O root.ca.pem http://www.symantec.com/content/en/us/enterprise/verisign/roots/
       VeriSign-Class%203-Public-Primary-Certification-Authority-G5.pem
   ```

   Run the following command to confirm that the root.ca.pem file is not empty:

   ```
   1 cat root.ca.pem
   ```

   If the root.ca.pem file is empty, check the wget URL and try again.

2. Use the following commands to start AWS Greengrass.

   ```
   1 cd /greengrass/ggc/core/
   2 sudo ./greengrassd start
   ```

You should see output similar to the following (note the PID number):

```
pi@raspberrypi:/greengrass/ggc/core $ sudo ./greengrassd start
Setting up greengrass daemon
Validating hardlink/softlink protection
Validating execution environment
Found cgroup subsystem: cpu
Found cgroup subsystem: cpuacct
Found cgroup subsystem: blkio
Found cgroup subsystem: memory
Found cgroup subsystem: devices
Found cgroup subsystem: freezer
Found cgroup subsystem: net_cls


Starting greengrass daemon
Greengrass successfully started with PID: 2244
```

Next, run the following command to confirm that the AWS Greengrass core software (daemon) is functioning. Replace *PID-number* with your own PID number:

```
1 ps aux | grep PID-number
```

You should see a path to the running AWS Greengrass daemon, as in **/greengrass/ggc/packages/1.5.0/ bin/daemon**. If you run into issues starting AWS Greengrass, see Troubleshooting AWS Greengrass Applications.

config.json Parameter Summary

The AWS Greengrass `config.json` file is contained in the **/greengrass/config** directory (or **/greengrass/ configuration** for AWS Greengrass version 1.0.0) and should be ready to go as-is. You can optionally review the contents of this file by running the following command (replace `config` with `configuration` for v1.0.0):

```
1 cat /greengrass/config/config.json
```

[GGC v1.5.0]

```
1  {
2      "coreThing": {
3          "caPath": "ROOT_CA_PEM_HERE",
4          "certPath": "CLOUD_PEM_CRT_HERE",
5          "keyPath": "CLOUD_PEM_KEY_HERE",
6          "thingArn": "THING_ARN_HERE",
7          "iotHost": "HOST_PREFIX_HERE.iot.AWS_REGION_HERE.amazonaws.com",
8          "ggHost": "greengrass.iot.AWS_REGION_HERE.amazonaws.com",
9          "keepAlive": 600
10     },
11     "runtime": {
12         "cgroup": {
13             "useSystemd": "yes|no"
14         }
15     },
16     "managedRespawn": true
17 }
```

The `config.json` file appears in `/greengrass/config/` and contains the following parameters:

Field	Description	Notes
caPath	The path to the AWS IoT root CA relative to the /greengrass/certs folder.	Save the file under the /greengrass/certs folder.
certPath	The path to the AWS Greengrass core certificate relative to the /greengrass/certs folder.	Save the file under the /greengrass/certs folder.
keyPath	The path to the AWS Greengrass core private key relative to /greengrass/certs folder.	Save the file under the /greengrass/certs folder.
thingArn	The Amazon Resource Name (ARN) of the AWS IoT thing that represents the AWS Greengrass core.	You can find it in the AWS Greengrass console under the definition for your AWS IoT thing.
iotHost	Your AWS IoT endpoint.	You can find it in the AWS IoT console under Settings.
ggHost	Your AWS endpoint.	You can find it in the AWS IoT console under Settings with greengrass. prepended.
keepAlive	The MQTT KeepAlive period, in seconds.	This is an optional value. The default value is 600 seconds.
useSystemd	A binary flag, if your device uses https://en.wikipedia.org/wiki/Systemd.	Values are yes or no. Use the dependency script in Module 1 to see if your device uses systemd.
managedRespawn	An optional over-the-air (OTA) updates feature, this indicates that the OTA agent needs to run custom code before an update.	For more information, see OTA Updates of AWS Greengrass Core Software.

[**GGC v1.3.0**]

```
1  {
2      "coreThing": {
3          "caPath": "ROOT_CA_PEM_HERE",
4          "certPath": "CLOUD_PEM_CRT_HERE",
5          "keyPath": "CLOUD_PEM_KEY_HERE",
6          "thingArn": "THING_ARN_HERE",
7          "iotHost": "HOST_PREFIX_HERE.iot.AWS_REGION_HERE.amazonaws.com",
8          "ggHost": "greengrass.iot.AWS_REGION_HERE.amazonaws.com",
9          "keepAlive": 600
10     },
11     "runtime": {
12         "cgroup": {
13             "useSystemd": "yes|no"
14         }
```

```
15    },
16    "managedRespawn": true
17  }
```

The `config.json` file appears in `/greengrass/config/` and contains the following parameters:

Field	Description	Notes
caPath	The path to the AWS IoT root CA relative to the `/greengrass/certs` folder.	Save the file under the `/greengrass/certs` folder.
certPath	The path to the AWS Greengrass core certificate relative to the `/greengrass/certs` folder.	Save the file under the `/greengrass/certs` folder.
keyPath	The path to the AWS Greengrass core private key relative to /greengrass/certs folder.	Save the file under the /greengrass/certs folder.
thingArn	The Amazon Resource Name (ARN) of the AWS IoT thing that represents the AWS Greengrass core.	You can find it in the AWS Greengrass console under the definition for your AWS IoT thing.
iotHost	Your AWS IoT endpoint.	You can find it in the AWS IoT console under Settings.
ggHost	Your AWS endpoint.	You can find it in the AWS IoT console under Settings with greengrass. prepended.
keepAlive	The MQTT KeepAlive period, in seconds.	This is an optional value. The default value is 600 seconds.
useSystemd	A binary flag, if your device uses https://en.wikipedia.org/wiki/Systemd.	Values are yes or no. Use the dependency script in Module 1 to see if your device uses systemd.
managedRespawn	An optional over-the-air (OTA) updates feature, this indicates that the OTA agent needs to run custom code before an update.	For more information, see OTA Updates of AWS Greengrass Core Software.

[GGC v1.1.0]

```
1   {
2     "coreThing": {
3       "caPath": "ROOT_CA_PEM_HERE",
4       "certPath": "CLOUD_PEM_CRT_HERE",
5       "keyPath": "CLOUD_PEM_KEY_HERE",
6       "thingArn": "THING_ARN_HERE",
7       "iotHost": "HOST_PREFIX_HERE.iot.AWS_REGION_HERE.amazonaws.com",
8       "ggHost": "greengrass.iot.AWS_REGION_HERE.amazonaws.com",
9       "keepAlive": 600
10    },
```

```
11      "runtime": {
12          "cgroup": {
13              "useSystemd": "yes|no"
14          }
15      }
16  }
```

The `config.json` file exists in `/greengrass/config/` and contains the following parameters:

Field	Description	Notes
caPath	The path to the AWS IoT root CA relative to the /greengrass/certs folder.	Save the file under the /greengrass/certs folder.
certPath	The path to the AWS Greengrass core certificate relative to the /greengrass/certs folder.	Save the file under the /greengrass/certs folder.
keyPath	The path to the AWS Greengrass core private key relative to the /greengrass/certs folder.	Save the file under the /greengrass/certs folder.
thingArn	The Amazon Resource Name (ARN) of the AWS IoT thing that represents the AWS Greengrass core.	You can find it in the AWS Greengrass console under the definition for your AWS IoT thing.
iotHost	Your AWS IoT endpoint.	You can find it in the AWS IoT console under Settings.
ggHost	Your AWS endpoint.	You can find it in the AWS IoT console under Settings with greengrass. prepended.
keepAlive	The MQTT KeepAlive period, in seconds.	This is an optional value. The default value is 600 seconds.
useSystemd	A binary flag, if your device uses https://en.wikipedia.org/wiki/Systemd.	Values are yes or no. Use the dependency script in Module 1 to see if your device uses systemd.

[GGC v1.0.0]

```
1  {
2      "coreThing": {
3          "caPath": "ROOT_CA_PEM_HERE",
4          "certPath": "CLOUD_PEM_CRT_HERE",
5          "keyPath": "CLOUD_PEM_KEY_HERE",
6          "thingArn": "THING_ARN_HERE",
7          "iotHost": "HOST_PREFIX_HERE.iot.AWS_REGION_HERE.amazonaws.com",
8          "ggHost": "greengrass.iot.AWS_REGION_HERE.amazonaws.com",
9          "keepAlive": 600
10      },
11      "runtime": {
```

```
12        "cgroup": {
13            "useSystemd": "yes|no"
14        }
15    }
16 }
```

The `config.json` file exists in `/greengrass/configuration/` and contains the following parameters:

Field	Description	Notes
caPath	The path to the AWS IoT root CA relative to the `/greengrass/configuration /certs` folder.	Save the file under the `/greengrass/configuration /certs` folder.
certPath	The path to the AWS Greengrass core certificate relative to the `/greengrass/ configuration/certs` folder.	Save the file under the /greengrass/configuration/certs folder.
keyPath	The path to the AWS Greengrass core private key relative to the /greengrass/configuration/certs folder.	Save the file under the /greengrass/configuration/certs folder.
thingArn	The Amazon Resource Name (ARN) of the AWS IoT thing that represents the AWS Greengrass core.	You can find it in the AWS Greengrass console under the definition for your AWS IoT hing.
iotHost	Your AWS IoT endpoint.	You can find it in the AWS IoT console under Settings.
ggHost	Your AWS endpoint.	You can find it in the AWS IoT console under **Settings** with `greengrass.` prepended.
keepAlive	The MQTT KeepAlive period, in seconds.	This is an optional value. The default value is 600 seconds.
useSystemd	A binary flag if your device uses https://en.wikipedia.org/wiki/Systemd.	Values are yes or no. Use the dependency script in Module 1 to see if your device uses systemd.

Module 3 (Part 1): Lambda Functions on AWS Greengrass

This module shows you how to configure a Lambda function and deploy it to your AWS Greengrass core device. It contains information about MQTT messaging, subscriptions, deployments on AWS Greengrass, and Lambda function configurations.

Part 1 of this module shows you how to deploy a Lambda function on the AWS Greengrass core that sends "Hello World" messages to the AWS Greengrass cloud. Part 2 covers the differences between on-demand and long-lived Lambda functions running on the AWS Greengrass core. Before you begin, make sure that you have completed Module 1 and Module 2 and have a running AWS Greengrass core device. Note that Module 3 (Part 1) and Module 3 (Part 2) should take approximately 30 minutes each.

Create and Package a Lambda Function

In order for a Python Lambda function to run on an AWS Greengrass core, it must be packaged with specific folders from the Python AWS Greengrass Core SDK. In the following, you will:

- Download the Python AWS Greengrass Core SDK to your computer (not the AWS Greengrass core device).
- Decompress the downloaded SDK file.
- Obtain the Python Lambda function (named `greengrassHelloWorld.py`) from the decompressed SDK.
- Create a Lambda function deployment package named `hello_world_python_lambda.zip` that contains `greengrassHelloWorld.py` and three required SDK folders.
- Upload the `hello_world_python_lambda.zip` package by using the Lambda console.
- Transfer the package to the AWS Greengrass core device by using the AWS Greengrass console.

1. In the AWS IoT console, choose **Software**.

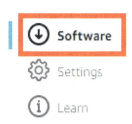

2. Under **SDKs**, for **AWS Greengrass Core SDK**, choose **Configure download**.

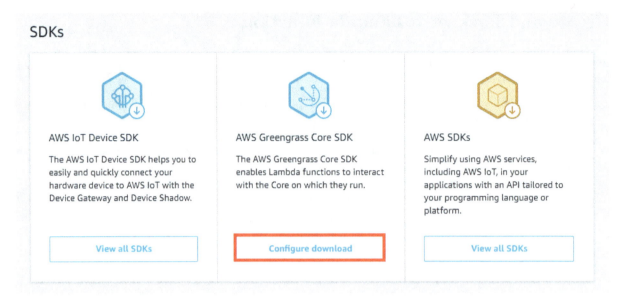

SDKs

AWS IoT Device SDK

The AWS IoT Device SDK helps you to easily and quickly connect your hardware device to AWS IoT with the Device Gateway and Device Shadow.

[View all SDKs]

AWS Greengrass Core SDK

The AWS Greengrass Core SDK enables Lambda functions to interact with the Core on which they run.

[Configure download]

AWS SDKs

Simplify using AWS services, including AWS IoT, in your applications with an API tailored to your programming language or platform.

[View all SDKs]

3. Choose **Python 2.7 version 1.1.0**, and then choose **Download Greengrass Core SDK**.

The AWS Greengrass Core SDK enables Lambda functions to interact with the Greengrass Core on which they run. This allows them to publish messages and interact with shadow data or invoke Lambda functions within the Greengrass Core.

Version 1.1.0   greengrass-core-python-sdk-1.1.0.tar.gz

[Python 2.7 version 1.1.0 ▾]   [**Download Greengrass Core SDK**]

4. Decompress the downloaded SDK. For instructions, choose the tab that corresponds to your operating system.

[Windows]

Use a tool for decompressing `.tar.gz` files on Windows such as 7-Zip, WinZip, or similar. As an example, the 7-Zip tool can be used to decompress `greengrass-core-python-sdk-1.1.0.tar.gz` as follows:

1. After installing 7-Zip, navigate to the `greengrass-core-python-sdk-1.1.0.tar.gz` file using Windows File Explorer (Windows logo key + E), right-click the file, choose **7-Zip**, then choose **Open archive**.

2. In the resulting 7-Zip window, double-click `greegrass-core-python-sdk-1.1.0.tar`, `aws_greengrass_core_sdk`, `examples`, `HelloWorld`, and then `greengrassHelloWorld.zip`.

3. Optionally using the Ctrl key, select the three SDK folders `greengrasssdk`, `greengrass_common`, `greengrass_ipc_python_sdk` and the Python `greengrassHelloWorld.py` Lambda file. Next, choose **Extract**, pick a location to extract the files to, and choose **OK**.

[macOS]

1. Using Finder, navigate to the `greengrass-core-python-sdk-1.1.0.tar.gz` file and double-click it. This creates the `aws_greengrass_core_sdk` folder.

2. Expand the `aws_greengrass_core_sdk` folder, then the `examples` folder, and then the `HelloWorld` folder.

3. Double-click the `greengrassHelloWorld.zip` file. This creates the `greengrassHelloWorld` folder – expand this folder.

[UNIX-like system]

1. Open a terminal window and navigate to the directory containing the `greengrass-core-python-sdk-1.1.0.tar.gz` file.

2. Run the following command to decompress the file:

```
1 sudo tar -xzf greengrass-core-python-sdk-1.1.0.tar.gz
```

This creates the `aws_greengrass_core_sdk` directory. Next, run the following commands:

```
1 cd /aws_greengrass_core_sdk/examples/HelloWorld
2 sudo unzip greengrassHelloWorld.zip
```

You use the three SDK folders (`greengrass_common`, `greengrass_ipc_python_sdk`, and `greengrasssdk`) and the Python `greengrassHelloWorld.py` Lambda function code in the next step.

Note that every five seconds, the `greengrassHelloWorld.py` Lambda function publishes one of two possible messages to the `hello/world` topic, as shown in the following code (to save space, all code comments have been removed):

```python
1 import greengrasssdk
2 import platform
3 from threading import Timer
4 import time
5
6 client = greengrasssdk.client('iot-data')
7 my_platform = platform.platform()
8
9 def greengrass_hello_world_run():
10     if not my_platform:
11         client.publish(topic='hello/world', payload='Hello world! Sent from Greengrass Core.')
12     else:
13         client.publish(topic='hello/world', payload='Hello world! Sent from Greengrass Core
                running on platform: {}'.format(my_platform))
14     Timer(5, greengrass_hello_world_run).start()
15
16 greengrass_hello_world_run()
17
18 def function_handler(event, context):
19     return
```

1. In order to run the Python `greengrassHelloWorld.py` Lambda function in the cloud, you must package it with the AWS Greengrass core SDK. Therefore, after you have extracted the SDK folders `greengrass_common`, `greengrass_ipc_python_sdk`, `greengrasssdk` and the `greengrassHelloWorld.py` Python Lambda file, package them into a compressed `.zip` file named `hello_world_python_lambda.zip`:

For UNIX-like systems (including the Mac terminal), this can be accomplished with the following command:

```
1 sudo zip -r hello_world_python_lambda.zip greengrass_common greengrass_ipc_python_sdk
    greengrasssdk greengrassHelloWorld.py
```

Note
Depending on your distribution, you may need to install `zip` first. For example, `sudo apt-get install zip` (this installation command may differ for your distribution).

Now you're ready to create your Lambda function and upload the function code.

1. Open the Lambda console and choose **Create function**.

2. Choose **Author from scratch**.

3. Name your function **Greengrass_HelloWorld**, and set the remaining fields as follows:

   - **Runtime** - choose **Python 2.7**.

   - **Role** - choose **Create new role from templates(s)**.

   - **Role name** - type a unique name for the role.

     Note that this role isn't used by AWS Greengrass, so you can optionally use any existing role.

Then, choose **Create function**.

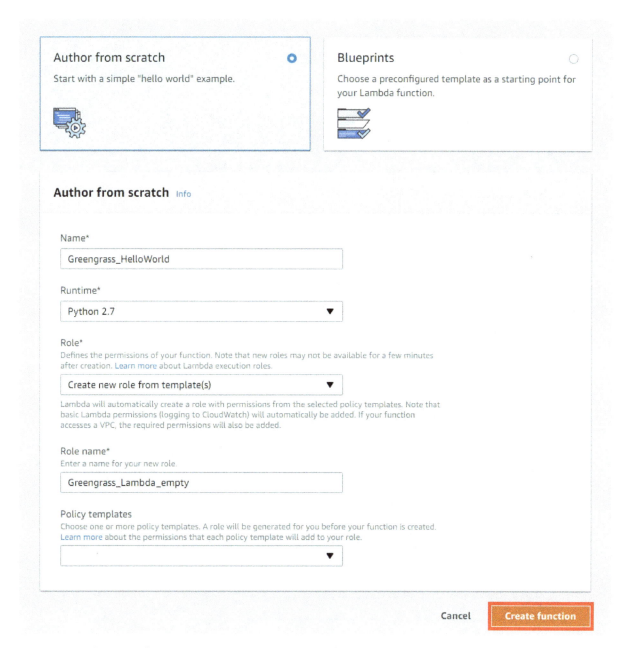

4. Upload your Lambda function deployment package, as follows:

    1. On the **Configuration** tab, under **Function code**, set the following fields:

        - **Code entry type** - choose **Upload a .ZIP file**.
        - **Runtime** - choose **Python 2.7**.
        - **Handler** - type **greengrassHelloWorld.function_handler**.

    2. Choose **Upload**, and then choose `hello_world_python_lambda.zip`. Your `hello_world_python_lambda.zip` file size may vary.

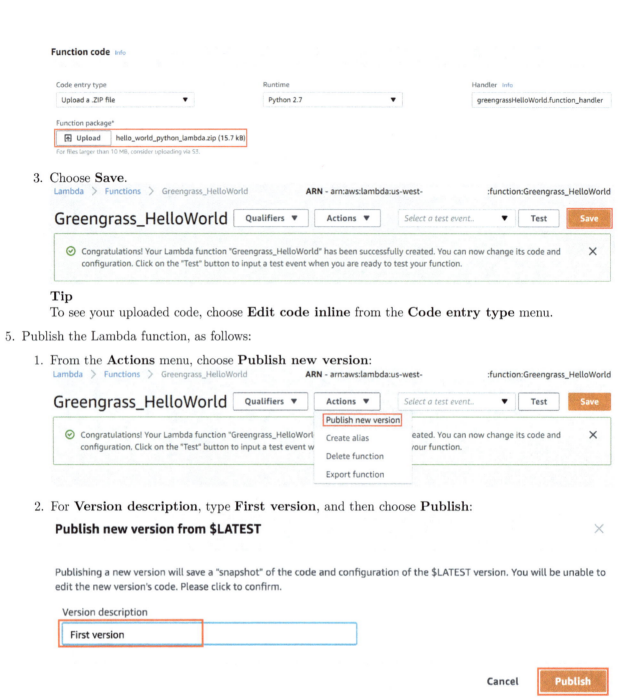

3. Choose **Save**.

> **Tip**
>
> To see your uploaded code, choose **Edit code inline** from the **Code entry type** menu.

5. Publish the Lambda function, as follows:

   1. From the **Actions** menu, choose **Publish new version**:

   2. For **Version description**, type **First version**, and then choose **Publish**:

6. Create an alias for the Lambda function version, as follows: **Note**
   Greengrass groups can reference a Lambda function by alias (recommended) or by version. Using an alias makes it easier to manage code updates because you don't have to change your subscription table or group definition when the function code is updated. Instead, you just point the alias to the new function version.

   1. From the **Actions** menu, choose **Create alias**.

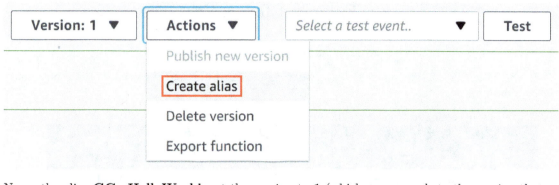

2. Name the alias **GG_HelloWorld**, set the version to **1** (which corresponds to the version that you just published), and then choose **Create**.

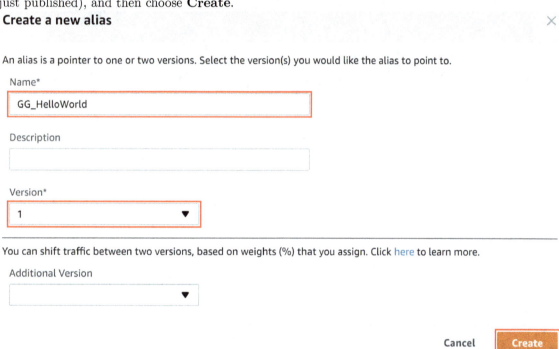

Note
AWS Greengrass doesn't support Lambda aliases for **$LATEST** versions.

Configure the Lambda Function for AWS Greengrass

You are now ready to configure your Lambda function for AWS Greengrass.

1. In the AWS IoT console, under **Greengrass**, choose **Groups**, and then choose the group that you created in Module 2.

2. On the group configuration page, choose **Lambdas**.

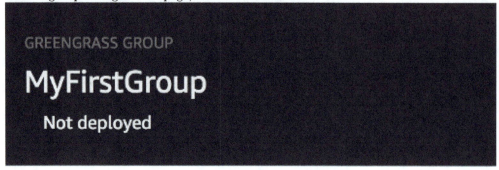

3. Choose **Add your first Lambda**.

Bring Lambda functions to the Edge

Greengrass allows you to extend Lambda functions to the edge. Lambda functions are small applications that can run on-demand or indefinitely. You can use local Lambda functions to respond to offline devices as you would with a connection to the Cloud.

Learn about local Lambda	Add your first Lambda

4. Choose **Use existing Lambda**.

Add a Lambda to your Greengrass Group

Local Lambdas are hosted on your Greengrass Core and connected to each other and devices by Subscriptions, but they can also be deployed individually to your Group.

Create a new Lambda function
You will be taken to the AWS Lambda Console and can author a new Lambda function.

Create new Lambda

Use an existing Lambda function
You will choose from a list of existing Lambda functions.

Use existing Lambda

5. Search for the name of the Lambda you created in the previous step (**Greengrass_HelloWorld**, not the alias name), select it, and then choose **Next**:

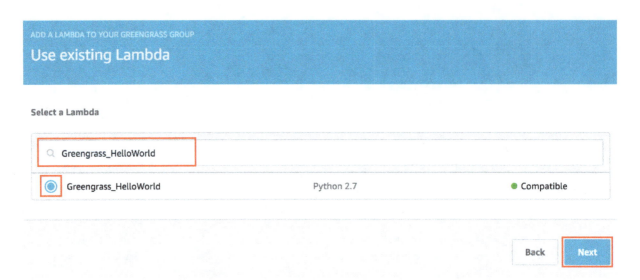

6. For the version, choose **Alias: GG_HelloWorld**, and then choose **Finish**. You should see the **Green-grass_HelloWorld** Lambda function in your group, using the **GG_HelloWorld** alias.

7. Choose the ellipsis (...) for the Lambda function, then choose **Edit Configuration**:

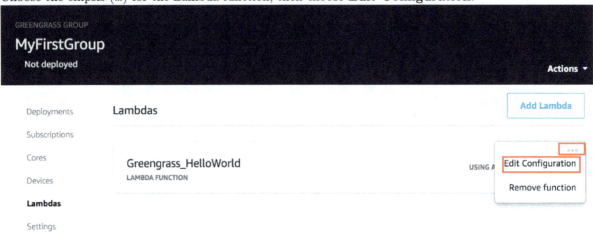

8. On the **Group-specific Lambda configuration** page, make the following changes:

   - For **Timeout** - set to 25 seconds. This Lambda function sleeps for 20 seconds before each invocation.
   - For **Lambda lifecycle** - select **Make this function long-lived and keep it running indefinitely**.

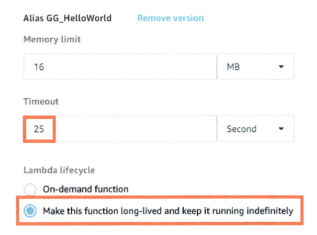

Alias GG_HelloWorld   Remove version

Memory limit

16	MB ▾

Timeout

25	Second ▾

Lambda lifecycle

⚪ On-demand function

🔘 Make this function long-lived and keep it running indefinitely

A *long-lived* Lambda function starts automatically after AWS Greengrass starts and keeps running in its own container (or sandbox). This is in contrast to an *on-demand* Lambda function which starts only when invoked and stops when there are no tasks left to execute. Information about long-lived and on-demand Lambda functions is provided in Module 3 (Part 2). **Note**

The Lambda function in this tutorial accepts **JSON** input payloads, but AWS Greengrass Lambda functions also support **Binary** input payloads. Binary support is especially useful when interacting with device data, because the restricted hardware capabilities of devices often make it difficult or impossible to construct a JSON data type.

9. Choose **Update** to save your changes to the Lambda function configuration.

10. An AWS Greengrass Lambda function can subscribe or publish messages (using the MQTT protocol):

   • To and from other devices (or device shadows) within the AWS Greengrass core. Information about device shadows is provided in Module 5.
   • To other Lambda functions.
   • To the AWS IoT cloud.

The AWS Greengrass group controls the way in which these components interact by using subscriptions that enable greater security and to provide predictable interactions.

A *subscription* consists of a source, target, and topic. The source is the originator of the message. The target is the destination of the message. The topic allows you to filter the data that is sent from the source to the target. The source or target can be an AWS Greengrass device, a Lambda function, a device shadow, or the AWS IoT cloud. A subscription is directed in the sense that messages flow in a specific direction. For an AWS Greengrass device to send messages to and receive messages from a Lambda function, you must set up two subscriptions: one from the device to the Lambda and another from the Lambda function to the device. The `Greengrass_HelloWorld` Lambda function sends messages only to the `hello/world` topic in the AWS IoT cloud, as shown in the following `greengrassHelloWorld.py` code snippet:

```
1 def greengrass_hello_world_run():
2     if not my_platform:
3         client.publish(topic='hello/world', payload='Hello world! Sent from Greengrass Core
             .')
4     else:
5         client.publish(topic='hello/world', payload='Hello world! Sent from Greengrass Core
                 running on platform: {}'.format(my_platform))
6
7     # Asynchronously schedule this function to be run again in 5 seconds
8     Timer(5, greengrass_hello_world_run).start()
9
10 # Execute the function above:
```

```
11  greengrass_hello_world_run()
```

Because the `Greengrass_HelloWorld` Lambda function sends messages only to the `hello/world` topic in the AWS IoT cloud, you only need to create one subscription from the Lambda function to the AWS IoT cloud, as shown next.

11. On the group configuration page, choose **Subscriptions**, and then choose **Add your first Subscription**.

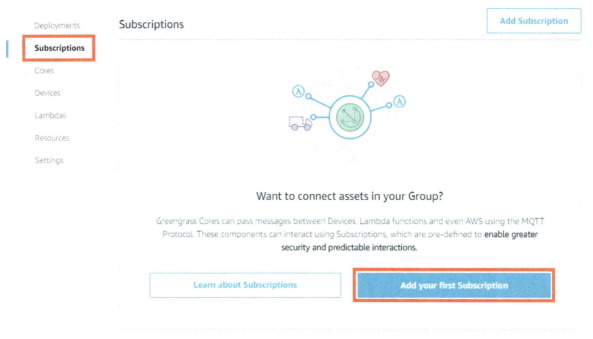

12. In the **Select a source** field, choose **Select**. Then, on the **Lambdas** tab, choose **Greengrass__HelloWorld** as the source.

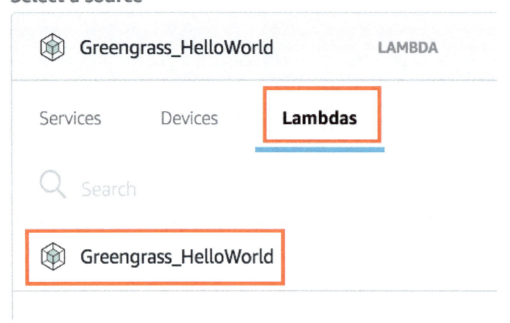

13. For the **Select a target** field, choose **Select**. Then, on the **Service** tab, choose **IoT Cloud**, and then

choose **Next**.

14. In the **Optional topic filter** field, type **hello/world**, then choose **Next**.

Source

| 🔷 Greengrass_HelloWorld | LAMBDA |

Optional topic filter   How do I enter a topic filter?

hello/world

Target

| 🔷 IoT Cloud | SERVICE |

Back   Next

15. Finally, choose **Finish**.

Deploy Cloud Configurations to an AWS Greengrass Core Device

1. Make sure that your AWS Greengrass core device is connected to the internet (for example, see if you can successfully navigate to a web page).

2. Make sure that the AWS Greengrass daemon is running on your core device. Run the following commands in your core device terminal.

   1. To check whether the daemon is running:

   ```
   1 ps aux | grep -E 'greengrass.*daemon'
   ```

   If the output contains a `root` entry for `/greengrass/ggc/packages/1.5.0/bin/daemon`, then the daemon is running.

   2. To start the daemon:

   ```
   1 cd /greengrass/ggc/core/
   2 sudo ./greengrassd start
   ```

   Now you're ready to deploy the Lambda function and subscription configurations to your AWS Greengrass core device.

3. In the AWS IoT console, on the group configuration page, from the **Actions** menu, choose **Deploy**.

4. On the **Configure how devices discover your core** page, choose **Automatic detection**. This enables devices to automatically acquire connectivity information for the core, such as IP address, DNS, and port number. Automatic detection is recommended, but AWS Greengrass also supports manually specified endpoints. You're only prompted for the discovery method the first time that the group is deployed.

   Automatically detect Core endpoints (recommended)

   Greengrass will detect and override connection information as it changes.

   | **Automatic detection** |

   Manually configure Core endpoints

   Manually manage connection information. This can be accessed via your Core device's settings.

   | Manually configure |

5. If prompted, choose **Grant permission** on the **Grant permission to access other services** page. This creates the Greengrass service role, which allows AWS Greengrass to access other AWS services on your behalf. This role is required for deployments to succeed. You need to do this only once per account.

The first deployment might take a few minutes. When the deployment is complete, you should see **Successfully completed** in the **Status** column on the **Deployments** page:

MyFirstGroup

● Successfully completed

Actions ▾

Deployments	Group history overview
Subscriptions	
Cores	
Devices	

By deployment ▾

Deployed	Version	Status	
Feb 28, 2018 4:58:48 PM -0800	21264da4-fd37-4005-89bc-eef04f693584	● Successfully completed	•••

Verify the Lambda Function Is Running on the Device

From the left pane of the AWS IoT console, choose **Test**.

 Monitor

 Onboard

 Manage

 Greengrass

 Secure

 Act

 Test

In **Subscription topic** field, type **hello/world** (don't choose **Subscribe to topic** yet). For **Quality of Service**, select **0**. For **MQTT payload display**, select **Display payloads as strings (more accurate)**.

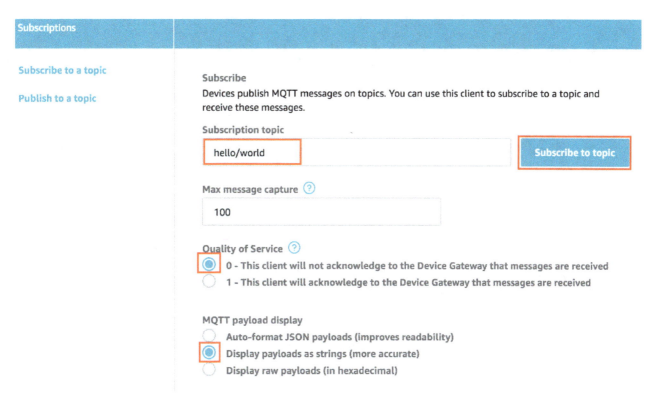

Next, choose **Subscribe to topic**.

Assuming the Lambda function is running on your device, it will publish messages to the **hello/world** topic similar to the following:

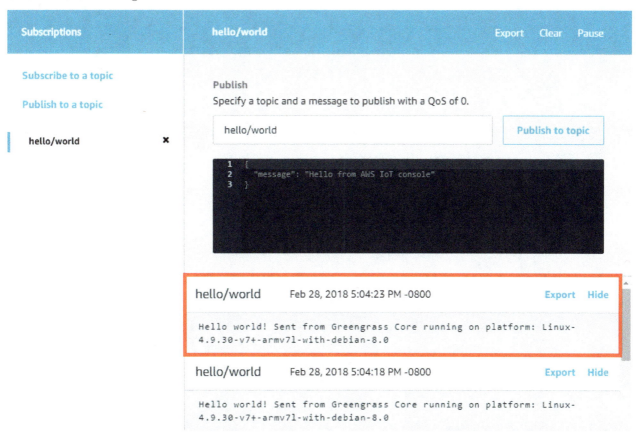

Note

Although the Lambda function running on the AWS Greengrass core device continues to send MQTT messages to the **hello/world** topic in the AWS IoT cloud, don't stop the AWS Greengrass daemon because the remaining modules assume that it's running.

Module 3 (Part 2): Lambda Functions on AWS Greengrass

This module shows you how to configure a Lambda function and deploy it to your AWS Greengrass core device. It contains information about MQTT messaging, subscriptions, deployments on AWS Greengrass, and Lambda function configurations.

Part 1 of this module described how to deploy a Lambda function on a AWS Greengrass core that sends "Hello World" messages to the AWS Greengrass cloud. This part explores the differences between on-demand and long-lived Lambda functions running on the AWS Greengrass core. Before you begin, make sure you have completed Module 1, Module 2, and Module 3 (Part 1). This module should take approximately 30 minutes to complete.

Create and Package the Lambda Function

1. Download the Lambda function code to your computer (not the Greengrass core device), as follows:

   1. In a web browser, open the greengrassHelloWorldCounter.py file on GitHub.

   2. Choose **Raw** to open the unformatted version of the file.

   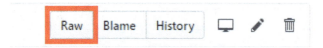

   3. Use Ctrl + S (or Command + S for the Mac) to save a copy of the `greengrassHelloWorldCounter`
      `.py` file. Save the file to the folder that contains the `greengrasssdk`, `greengrass_common`, and
      `greengrass_ipc_python_sdk` SDK folders. **Note**
      For UNIX-like systems, you can run the following Terminal command to download the
      `greengrassHelloWorldCounter.py` file:

```
1  sudo wget https://raw.githubusercontent.com/aws-samples/aws-greengrass-samples/master/hello
   -world-counter-python/greengrassHelloWorldCounter.py
```

2. Package the `greengrassHelloWorldCounter.py` file with the three SDK folders into a `.zip` file, as
   described in Module 3 (Part 1). Name the package **hello_world_counter_python_lambda.zip**.

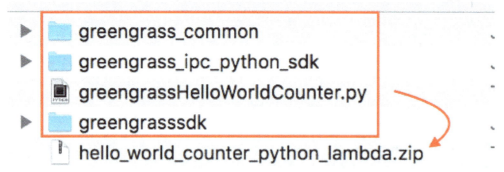

3. In the Lambda console, create a Python 2.7 function named **Greengrass_HelloWorld_Counter**, as
   described in Module 3 (Part 1). You can use the existing role.

4. Upload your Lambda function deployment package, as follows:

   1. On the **Configuration** tab, under **Function code**, set the following fields:

      - **Code entry type** - choose **Upload a .ZIP file**.
      - **Runtime** - choose **Python 2.7**.
      - **Handler** - type **greengrassHelloWorldCounter.function_handler**.

   2. Choose **Upload**, and then choose `hello_world_counter_python_lambda.zip`.

3. At the top of the page, choose **Save**.

5. Publish the first version of the function, as follows:

    1. From the **Actions** menu, choose **Publish new version**. For **Version description**, type **First version**.

    2. Choose **Publish**.

6. Create an alias for the function version, as follows:

    1. From the **Actions** menu, choose **Create alias**, and set the following values:

        - **Name** - type **GG_HW_Counter**.
        - **Version** - choose **1**.

    2. Choose **Create**.

Create a new alias

An alias is a pointer to one or two versions. Select the version(s) you would like the alias to point to.

Name*

GG_HW_Counter

Description

Version*

1 ▼

Cancel   Create

Recall that aliases create a single entity for your Lambda function that AWS Greengrass devices can subscribe to without having to update subscriptions with Lambda version numbers every time the function is modified.

Configure Long-Lived Lambda Functions for AWS Greengrass

You are now ready to configure your Lambda function for AWS Greengrass.

1. In the AWS IoT console, under **Greengrass**, choose **Groups**, and then choose the group that you created in Module 2.

2. On the group configuration page, choose **Lambdas**, and then choose **Add Lambda**.

3. On the **Add a Lambda to your Greengrass Group** page, choose **Use existing Lambda**.

4. On the **Use existing Lambda page**, choose **Greengrass_HelloWorld_Counter**, and then choose **Next**.

5. On the **Select a Lambda version** page, choose **Alias: GG_HW_Counter**, and then choose **Finish**.

6. On the **Lambdas** page, from the **Greengrass_HelloWorld_Counter** menu, choose **Edit Configuration**.

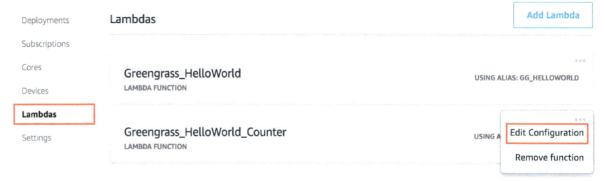

7. On the configuration page, edit the following properties:

   - **Timeout** - set to 25 seconds. This Lambda function sleeps for 20 seconds before each invocation.
   - **Lambda lifecycle** - choose **Make this function long-lived and keep it running indefinitely**.

Greengrass_HelloWorld_Counter

View function in AWS Lambda

Alias GG_HW_Counter

Memory limit

16	MB ▼

Timeout

25	Sec... ▼

Lambda lifecycle

◯ On-demand function

🔘 Make this function long-lived and keep it running indefinitely

8. Choose **Update**.

Test Long-Lived Lambda Functions

A *long-lived Lambda function* starts automatically when the AWS Greengrass core starts (and runs in a single container or sandbox). Any variables or preprocessing that are defined outside of the function handler are retained for every invocation of the function handler. Multiple invocations of the function handler are queued until earlier invocations have been executed. The greengrassHelloWorldCounter.py Lambda function is similar to the greengrassHelloWorld.py function except there is a variable, my_counter, that is outside of the function_handler(event, context) method (code comments were removed for brevity):

```
1  import greengrasssdk
2  import platform
3  import time
4  import json
5
6  client = greengrasssdk.client('iot-data')
7
8  my_platform = platform.platform()
9
10 my_counter = 0
11
12 def function_handler(event, context):
13     global my_counter
14     my_counter = my_counter + 1
15     if not my_platform:
16         client.publish(
17             topic='hello/world/counter',
18             payload=json.dumps({'message': 'Hello world! Sent from Greengrass Core.  Invocation
                 Count: {}'.format(my_counter)})
19         )
20     else:
21         client.publish(
22             topic='hello/world/counter',
23             payload=json.dumps({'message': 'Hello world! Sent from Greengrass Core running on
                 platform: {}.  Invocation Count: {}'
24                                 .format(my_platform, my_counter)})
25         )
26     time.sleep(20)
27     return
```

1. On the group configuration page, choose **Subscriptions**, then **Add Subscription**. Under **Select a source**, choose the **Lambdas** tab, then choose **Greengrass_HelloWorld_Counter**. Next, under **Select a target**, choose the **Services** tab, choose **IoT Cloud**, and then choose **Next**.

Select your source and target

A Subscription consists of a source, target, and topic. The source is the originator of the message. The target is the destination of the message. The first step is selecting your source and target.

Select a source

📦 Greengrass_HelloWorld_Counter	LAMBDA	Edit

Select a target

🔷 IoT Cloud	SERVICE	Edit

Back   **Next**

For **Optional topic filter**, type **hello/world/counter**. Choose **Next** and then choose **Finish**.

Source

📦 Greengrass_HelloWorld_Counter	LAMBDA

Optional topic filter   How do I enter a topic filter?

hello/world/counter

Target

🔷 IoT Cloud	SERVICE

Back   **Next**

This single subscription goes in one direction only: from the **Greengrass_HelloWorld_Counter** Lambda function to the AWS IoT cloud. To trigger this Lambda function from the cloud, you need to create a subscription in the opposite direction.

2. Add another subscription with **IoT Cloud** as the source and **Greengrass_HelloWorld_Counter** as the target. Use the **hello/world/counter/trigger** topic:

71

Note the **/trigger** extension above – because you have created two subscriptions, you do not want them to interfere with each other.

3. Make sure that the AWS Greengrass daemon is running, as described in Deploy Cloud Configurations to a Core Device.

Note that with the daemon running, the prior `greengrassHelloWorld.py` Lambda function will continue to send messages to the `hello/world` topic (in the AWS IoT cloud). This does not, however, interfere with the messages sent from the `greengrassHelloWorldCounter.py` Lambda function to the AWS IoT cloud, since they're directed to a different topic, namely `hello/world/counter`.

4. On the group configuration page, from the **Actions** menu, choose **Deploy** to deploy the updated group configuration to your AWS Greengrass core device.

5. After your deployment is complete, in the AWS IoT console, choose **Test**. In **Subscription topic**, type **hello/world/counter**. For **Quality of Service**, select **0**. For **MQTT payload display**, select **Display payloads as strings**, and then choose **Subscribe to topic**.

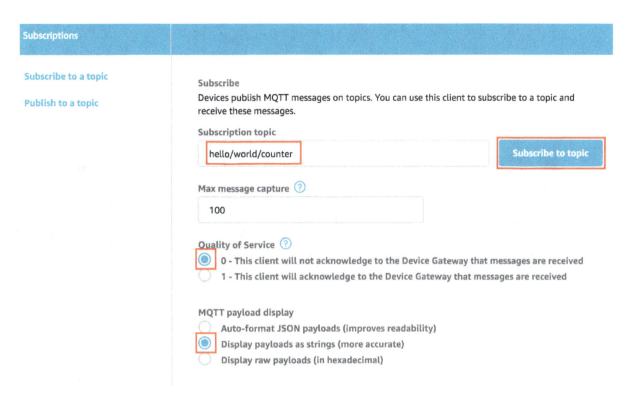

Unlike Part 1 of this module, you should *not* be able to see any messages after you subscribe to `hello/world/counter`. This is because the `greengrassHelloWorldCounter.py` code to publish to the topic `hello/world/counter` is inside the `function_handler(event, context)` function, and `function_handler(event, context)` is triggered only when it receives an MQTT message on the **hello/world/counter/trigger** topic. To help further explain this, consider the **greengrass_HelloWorld_Counter** related subscriptions:

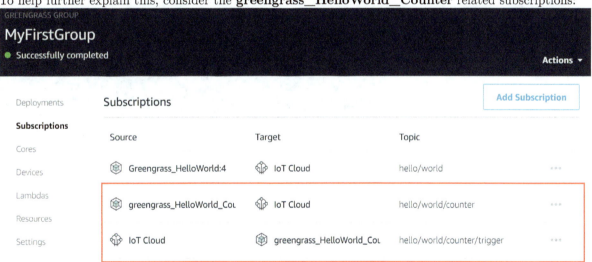

In the second row, we see that the **greengrass_HelloWorld_Counter** Lambda function can send messages to the **IoT Cloud** on the **hello/world/counter** topic. In the third row, we see that the **IoT Cloud** will can send messages to the **greengrass_HelloWorld_Counter** Lambda function when that message is sent to the **hello/world/counter/trigger** topic (note that there is nothing special about the word **trigger**). The **greengrass_HelloWorld_Counter** Lambda function ignores these sent messages and merely runs the code within `function_handler(event, context)`, which sends a message back to the **hello/world/counter** topic in the AWS IoT cloud (see the prior `greengrassHelloWorldCounter.py` code listing).

So, to trigger the `function_handler(event, context)` handler, publish any message (the default message is fine) to the **hello/world/counter/trigger** topic, as shown next.

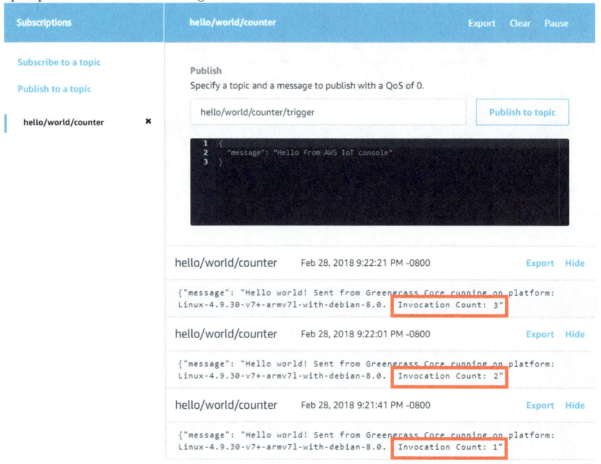

Every time a message is published to the `hello/world/counter/trigger` topic, the `my_counter` variable is incremented (see `Invocation Count` in the following). Because the function handler in the Lambda function includes a 20-second sleep cycle (i.e., `time.sleep(20)`), repeatedly triggering the handler queues up responses from the AWS Greengrass core.

Test On-Demand Lambda Functions

An *on-demand Lambda function* is similar in functionality to an AWS cloud Lambda function. Multiple invocations of an on-demand Lambda function can run in parallel. Each invocation of the Lambda function creates a new, separate container to process invocations. The container can be reused for future invocations if resources permit. For information about container reuse, see Understanding Container Reuse in AWS Lambda. Any variables or preprocessing that are defined outside of the function handler are not retained when new containers are created. As a best practice, we recommend that you use on-demand Lambda functions instead of long-lived functions whenever possible because they are less resource-intensive.

1. On the group configuration page, choose **Lambdas**. For the **Greengrass_HelloWorld_Counter** Lambda function, choose **Edit Configuration**.

2. Under **Lambda lifecycle**, select **On-demand function**.

Next, choose **Update**.

3. On the group configuration page, from the **Actions** menu, choose **Deploy** to deploy the updated group

configuration to your AWS Greengrass core device.

4. After your deployment is complete, in the AWS IoT console, choose **Test**. For **Subscription topic**, type **hello/world/counter**. For **Quality of Service**, select **0**. For **MQTT payload display**, select **Display payloads as strings** and then choose **Subscribe to topic**.

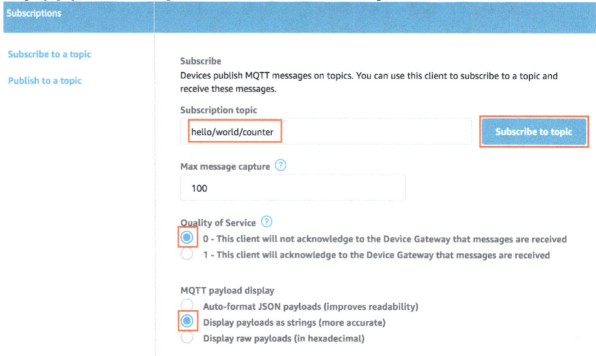

Again, you should not be able to see any messages after you subscribe. Trigger the function to the **hello/world/counter/trigger** topic by sending any message (the default message is fine), then choose **Publish to topic** three times, *within five seconds* of each press of the button.

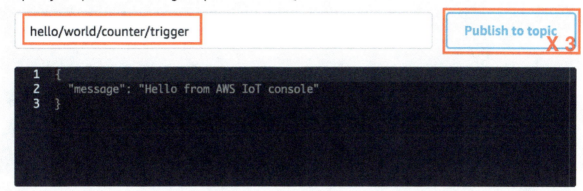

Each publish is triggering the function handler and creating a new container for each invocation. The invocation count is not incremented for each of the three times you triggered the function because each on-demand Lambda function has its own container/sandbox.

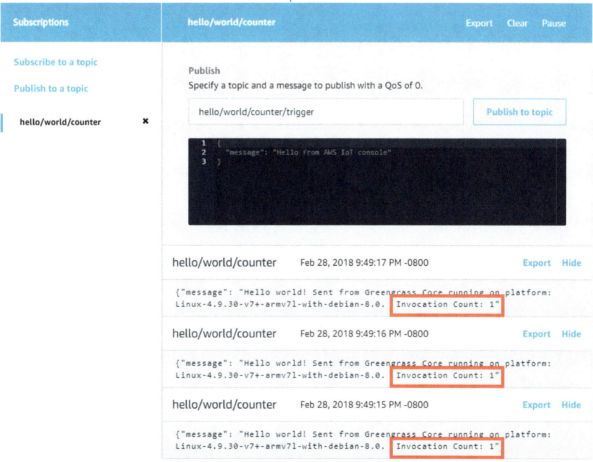

Wait approximately thirty seconds or more, and then choose **Publish to topic**. This time you should see an incremented invocation count.

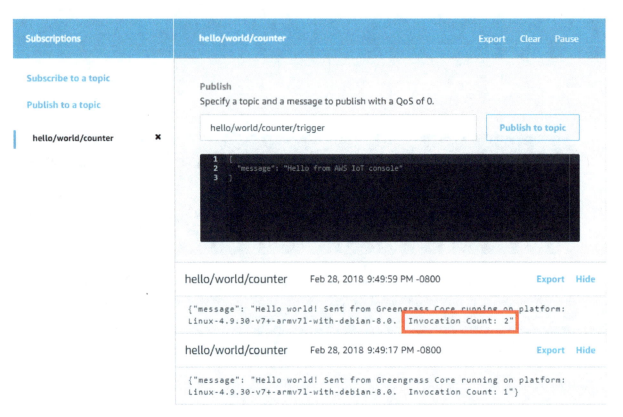

This shows that a container, first created from a prior invocation, is being reused, and preprocessing variables outside of the function handler have been stored.

You should now understand the two types of Lambda functions that can run on the AWS Greengrass core. The next module, Module 4, shows you how devices can interact within an AWS Greengrass group.

Module 4: Interacting with Devices in an AWS Greengrass Group

This module shows you how AWS IoT devices can connect to and communicate with an AWS Greengrass core device. AWS IoT devices that connect to an AWS Greengrass core are part of an AWS Greengrass group and can participate in the AWS Greengrass programming paradigm. In this module, one AWS Greengrass device sends a "Hello World" message to another AWS Greengrass device within the AWS Greengrass group:

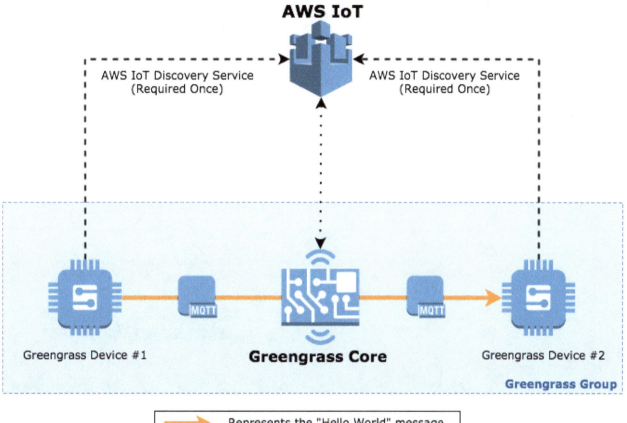

Before you begin, make sure that you have completed Module 1, Module 2, Module 3 (Part 1), and Module 3 (Part 2). You do not need other components or devices. This module should take less than 30 minutes to complete.

Create AWS IoT Devices in an AWS Greengrass Group

1. In the AWS IoT console, choose **Greengrass**, choose **Groups**, and then choose your group to open its configuration page. Next, choose **Devices** and then choose **Add your first Device**.

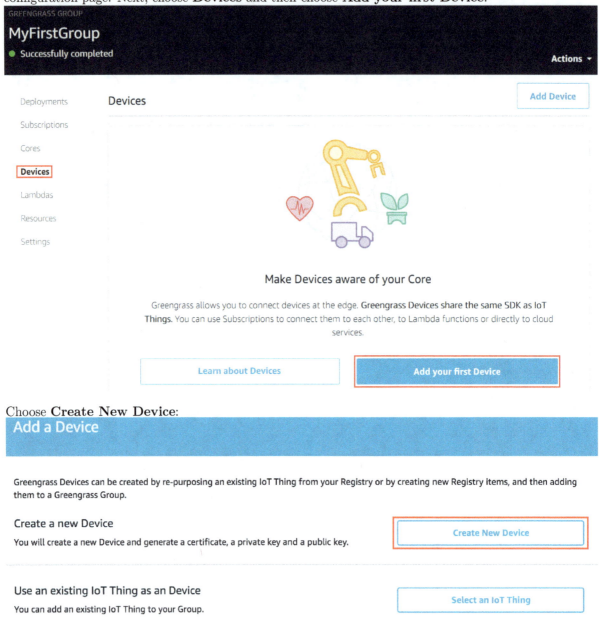

Choose **Create New Device**:

Register this device as **HelloWorld_Publisher**, then choose **Next**:

Create a Registry entry for a device

Every Greengrass Group requires a device running Greengrass software. It enables communication between Devices, local Lambda functions, and AWS cloud computing services. Adding information to the Registry is the first step in provisioning a device as your Greengrass Core.

Name

HelloWorld_Publisher

Show optional configuration (this can be done later) ▼

Back   Next

For **1-Click**, choose **Use Defaults**:

Set up security

The Device needs a certificate and a policy before it can be added to Greengrass. If you're unfamiliar with any of these steps we recommend the Automated Setup.

1-Click

This will generate a certificate, public key and private key using AWS IoT's root CA, generate a default policy, and create a new IAM role with default permissions.

Use Defaults

Advanced setup

This will allow you to handle certificate signing request (CSR) based on a private key you own, customize your own policy, and use an existing IAM role or create a new one.

Customize

Create a folder on your computer.

Download the certificates for your device into the folder, and then decompress them (to decompress `tar.gz` files on Windows, see the **Windows** tab in step 2 of Create and Package a Lambda Function).

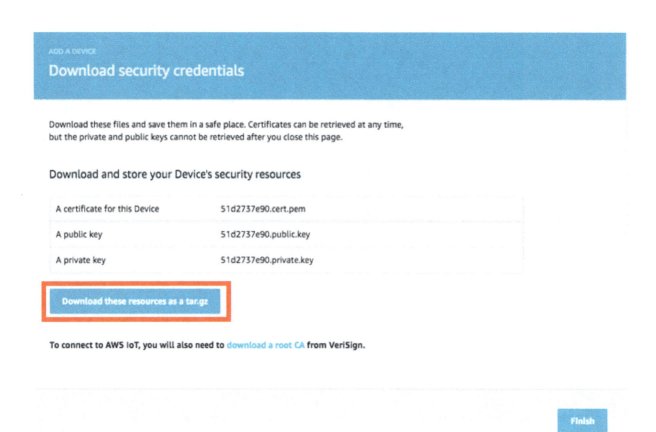

Note the common GUID-like filename component for the **HelloWorld_Publisher** device (in this example, `51d2737e90`), this will be needed later. Finally, choose **Finish**.

2. By choosing **Add Device**, repeat step 1 to add another device to the group and name it **HelloWorld_Subscriber**. Download the certificates for your second device onto your computer as well, saving them in the same folder as the first set of certificates. Choose **Finish**. Again, note the common GUID-like filename component for the **HelloWorld_Subscriber** device.

You should now have two devices in your AWS Greengrass group:

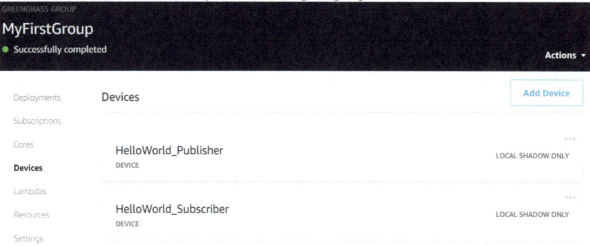

3. Download another AWS IoT root certificate from Symantec and save it as `root-ca-cert.pem` in the folder you just created. For this module, this certificate and the certificates and keys for both devices should be in one folder on your computer (not on the AWS Greengrass core device). **Note**

If you're using a web browser on the Mac and you receive a This certificate is already installed as a certificate authority alert, you can open a Terminal window and run the following commands to download the certificate into the folder containing the HelloWorld_Publisher and HelloWorld_Subscriber device certificates/keys:

```
1  cd path-to-folder-containing-device-certificates
2  curl -o ./root-ca-cert.pem http://www.symantec.com/content/en/us/enterprise/verisign/roots/
     VeriSign-Class%203-Public-Primary-Certification-Authority-G5.pem
```

Run `cat root-ca-cert.pem` to ensure that the file is not empty. If so, check the URL and try the `curl` command again.

Configure Subscriptions

In this step, you create a subscription that enables the GG_TrafficLight shadow to send updated states to the GG_Car_Aggregator Lambda function. This subscription is in addition to the subscriptions that you created in Module 5, which are all required for this module.

1. On the group configuration page, choose **Subscriptions**, and then choose **Add Subscription**.

2. On the **Select your source and target** page, set the following values:

   - **Select a source** - choose **Services** and then choose **Local Shadow Service**.
   - **Select a target** - choose **Lambdas** and then choose **GG_Car_Aggregator**.

   Choose **Next**.

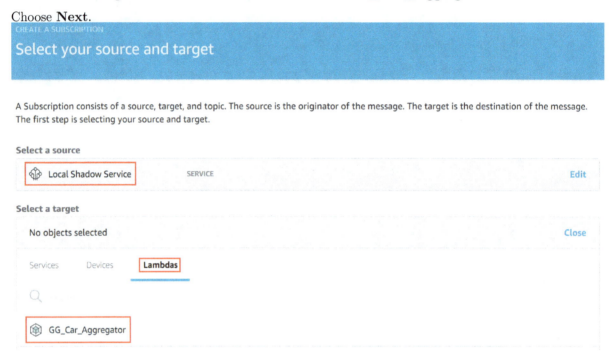

3. On the **Filter your data with a topic** page, for **Optional topic filter**, type **$aws/things/GG_TrafficLight/shadow/update/documents**.

   Choose **Next**, and then choose **Finish**.

Note

On the **Subscriptions** page, the target displays the names of the function version and the alias: **GG_Car_Aggregator:GG_CarAggregator**.

The following table shows the complete list of subscriptions that this module requires. The new shadow subscription appears in the last row of the table. You created the other subscriptions in Module 5.

[See the AWS documentation website for more details] **Note**

Except for Module 5, you can delete the subscriptions from earlier modules that are not included in the table.

1. Make sure that the AWS Greengrass daemon is running, as described in Deploy Cloud Configurations to a Core Device.

2. On the group configuration page, from the **Actions** menu, choose **Deploy** to deploy the updated group configuration to your AWS Greengrass core device.

Install the AWS IoT Device SDK for Python

The AWS IoT Device SDK for Python can be used by all AWS IoT devices to communicate with the AWS IoT cloud and AWS Greengrass core devices (using the Python programming language). Note that the SDK requires Python 2, version 2.7+ or Python 3, version 3.3+. Additionally, the SDK requires OpenSSL version 1.0.1+ (TLS version 1.2) compiled with the Python executable.

To install the SDK onto your computer, with all required components, choose the appropriate tab:

[**Windows**]

1. Open an elevated command prompt and run the following command:

```
1 python --version
```

If no version information is returned or if the version number is less than 2.7 for Python 2 or less than 3.3 for Python 3, then install Python 2.7+ or Python 3.3+ by following the instructions in Downloading Python. For additional information, see Using Python on Windows (note the Python version number drop-down menu).

2. Using a web browser, download the AWS IoT Device SDK for Python zip file and and save it as **aws-iot-device-sdk-python-latest.zip** (this should be the default name). The **zip** file will typically be saved to your **Downloads** folder. Decompress **aws-iot-device-sdk-python-latest.zip** to an appropriate location, such as your home directory (i.e., **cd %HOME%**). Note the file path to the decompressed **aws-iot-device-sdk-python-latest** folder. In the next step, this file path will be indicated by *path-to-SDK-folder*.

3. From the elevated command prompt, run the following:

```
1 cd path-to-SDK-folder
2 python setup.py install
```

[**macOS**]

1. Open a Terminal window and run the following command:

```
1 python --version
```

If no version information is returned or if the version number is less that 2.7 for Python 2 or less than 3.3 for Python 3, then install Python 2.7+ or Python 3.3+ by following the instructions in Downloading Python. For additional information, see Using Python on a Macintosh (note the Python version number drop-down menu).

2. In the Terminal window, run the following commands to determine the OpenSSL version:

```
1 python
2 >>> import ssl
3 >>> print ssl.OPENSSL_VERSION
```

Note the OpenSSL version value. **Note**
Use **print(ssl.OPENSSL_VERSION)** if you're running Python 3.

To close the Python shell, run the following command:

```
1 >>> exit()
```

If the OpenSSL version is 1.0.1 or later, skip to step 3. Otherwise, proceed as follows:

1. From the Terminal window, run the following command to determine if the computer is using Simple Python Version Management:

```
1 which pyenv
```

If a file path is returned, then choose the **Using pyenv** tab. If nothing is returned, choose the **Not using pyenv** tab.

[Using pyenv]

1. See Python Releases for Max OS X (or similar) to determine the latest stable Python version. In the following, this value shall be indicated by *latest-Python-version*.

2. From the Terminal window, run the following commands:

```
1 pyenv install latest-Python-version
2 pyenv global latest-Python-version
```

For example, if the latest version for Python 2 is 2.7.14, then these commands would be:

```
1 pyenv install 2.7.14
2 pyenv global 2.7.14
```

3. Close the Terminal window, then reopen it.

4. In the reopened Terminal window, run the following commands:

```
1 python
2 >>> import ssl
3 >>> print ssl.OPENSSL_VERSION
```

The OpenSSL version should be at least 1.0.1. If the version is less than 1.0.1, then the update failed – check the Python version value used in the prior `pyenv install` and `pyenv global` commands and try again.

5. Run the following command to exit the Python shell:

```
1 >>> exit()
```

[Not using pyenv]

1. From a Terminal window, run the following command to determine if brew is installed:

```
1 which brew
```

If a file path is not returned, install `brew` as follows:

```
1 /usr/bin/ruby -e "$(curl -fsSL https://raw.githubusercontent.com/Homebrew/install/master/
    install)"
```

Note
Follow the installation prompts and be aware that the download for the Xcode command line tools can take some time.

1. Run the following commands:

```
1 brew update
2 brew install openssl
3 brew install python@2
```

Recall that the AWS IoT Device SDK for Python requires OpenSSL version 1.0.1 (or later) compiled with the Python executable. The prior `brew install python` command installs a `python2` executable that meets this requirement. The `python2` executable is installed in the `/usr/local/bin` directory, which should be part of the `PATH` environment variable. To confirm this, run the following command:

```
1 python2 --version
```

If `python2` version information is provided, skip to the next step. Otherwise, permanently add the `/usr/local/bin` path to your `PATH` environment variable by appending the following line to your shell profile:

```
1 export PATH="/usr/local/bin:$PATH"
```

For example, if you're using `.bash_profile` or do not yet have a shell profile, run the following command from a Terminal window:

```
1 echo 'export PATH="/usr/local/bin:$PATH"' >> ~/.bash_profile
```

Next, source your shell profile and confirm that `python2 --version` provides version information. For example, if you're using `.bash_profile`, run the following commands:

```
1 source ~/.bash_profile
2 python2 --version
```

`python2` version information should be returned.

2. Append the following line to your shell profile:

```
1 alias python="python2"
```

For example, if you're using `.bash_profile` or do not yet have a shell profile, run the following command:

```
1 echo 'alias python="python2"' >> ~/.bash_profile
```

3. Next, source your shell profile. For example, if you're using `.bash_profile`, run the following command:

```
1 source ~/.bash_profile
```

Now, invoking the `python` command will run the Python executable containing the required OpenSSL version (i.e., `python2`) .

4. Run the following commands:

```
1 python
2 >>> import ssl
3 >>> print ssl.OPENSSL_VERSION
```

The OpenSSL version should be 1.0.1 or later.

5. To exit the Python shell, run the following command:

```
1 >>> exit()
```

---

1. Run the following commands to install the AWS IoT Device SDK for Python:

```
1 cd ~
2 git clone https://github.com/aws/aws-iot-device-sdk-python.git
3 cd aws-iot-device-sdk-python
4 python setup.py install
```

[UNIX-like system]

1. From a terminal window, run the following command:

```
1 python --version
```

If no version information is returned or if the version number is less that 2.7 for Python 2 or less than 3.3 for Python 3, then install Python 2.7+ or Python 3.3+ by following the instructions in Downloading Python. For additional information, see Using Python on Unix platforms (note the Python version number drop-down menu)

2. In the terminal, run the following commands to determine the OpenSSL version:

```
1 python
2 >>> import ssl
3 >>> print ssl.OPENSSL_VERSION
```

Note the OpenSSL version value.

To close the Python shell, run the following command:

```
1 >>> exit()
```

If the OpenSSL version is 1.0.1 or later, skip to the next step. Otherwise, run the command(s) to update OpenSSL for your distribution. For example, sudo yum update openssl, sudo apt-get update, etc.

Confirm that the OpenSSL version is 1.0.1 or later by running the following commands:

```
1 python
2 >>> import ssl
3 >>> print ssl.OPENSSL_VERSION
4 >>> exit()
```

3. Run the following commands to install the AWS IoT Device SDK for Python:

```
1 cd ~
2 git clone https://github.com/aws/aws-iot-device-sdk-python.git
3 cd aws-iot-device-sdk-python
4 sudo python setup.py install
```

After the AWS IoT Device SDK for Python is installed, navigate to the SDK's samples folder, the greengrass folder, and then copy the basicDiscovery.py file to the folder containing the **HelloWorld_Publisher** and **HelloWorld_Subscriber** device certificates files, as shown in the following example (the GUID-like filename components will be different):

- 112dd2e43f.cert.pem
- 112dd2e43f.private.key
- 112dd2e43f.public.key
- basicDiscovery.py
- e1f3dd683e.cert.pem
- e1f3dd683e.private.key
- e1f3dd683e.public.key
- root-ca-cert.pem

Test Communications

1. On your computer, open two command-line windows. Just as in Module 5, one window will be for the GG_Switch device and the other for the GG_TrafficLight device. **Note** These are the same commands that you ran in Module 5.

   Run the following commands for the GG_Switch device:

```
1 cd path-to-certs-folder
2 python lightController.py --endpoint AWS_IOT_ENDPOINT --rootCA root-ca-cert.pem --cert
    switch.cert.pem --key switch.private.key --thingName GG_TrafficLight --clientId
    GG_Switch
```

   Run the following commands for the GG_TrafficLight device:

```
1 cd path-to-certs-folder
2 python trafficLight.py --endpoint AWS_IOT_ENDPOINT --rootCA root-ca-cert.pem --cert light.
    cert.pem --key light.private.key --thingName GG_TrafficLight --clientId GG_TrafficLight
```

   Every 20 seconds, the switch updates the shadow state to G, Y, and R, and the light displays its new state.

2. On every third green light (every 3 minutes), the function handler of the Lambda function is triggered, and a new DynamoDB record is created. After `lightController.py` and `trafficLight.py` have run for three minutes, go to the AWS Management Console, search for and open the DynamoDB console. Make sure that the **N. Virgina** (`us-east-1`) region is selected, then choose **Tables** and choose the **CarStats** table. Next, choose the **Items** tab:

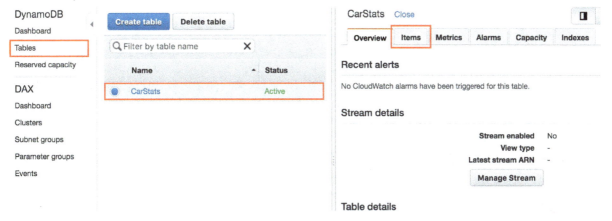

   You should see entries with basic statistics on cars passed (one entry for every three minutes). You may need to choose the refresh button (two circular arrows) to view updates to the **CarStats** table:

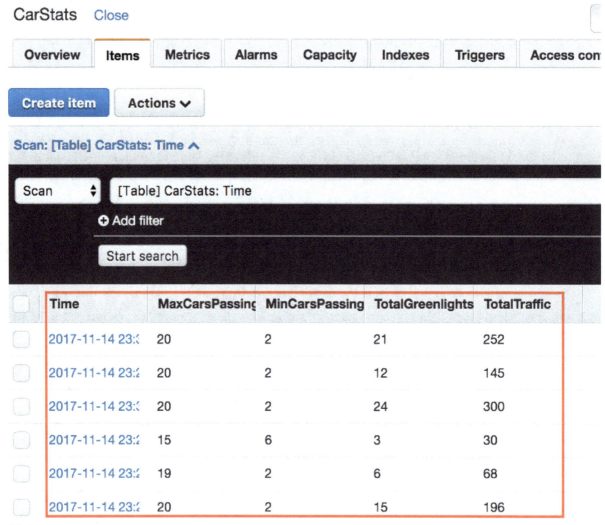

Note
If necessary, you can troubleshoot issues by viewing the AWS Greengrass core logs, particularly `router.log`:

```
1 cd /greengrass/ggc/var/log
2 sudo cat system/router.log | more
```

For more information, see Troubleshooting AWS Greengrass Applications.

You have reached the end of this tutorial and should now understand the AWS Greengrass programming model and its fundamental concepts, including AWS Greengrass cores, groups, subscriptions, and the deployment process for Lambda functions running at the edge.

You can delete the DynamoDB table, delete the Lambda functions, and stop communications between the AWS Greengrass core device and the AWS IoT cloud. To stop communications, open a terminal on the AWS Greengrass core device and run **one** of the following commands:

- To shut down the AWS Greengrass core device:

```
1 sudo halt
```

- To stop the AWS Greengrass daemon:

```
1 cd /greengrass/ggc/core/
2 sudo ./greengrassd stop
```

Module 5: Interacting with Device Shadows

This advanced module shows you how AWS Greengrass devices can interact with AWS IoT device shadows in an AWS Greengrass group. A *shadow* is a JSON document that is used to store current or desired state information for a thing. In this module, you discover how one AWS Greengrass device (`GG_Switch`) can modify the state of another AWS Greengrass device (`GG_TrafficLight`) and how these states can be synced to the AWS Greengrass cloud:

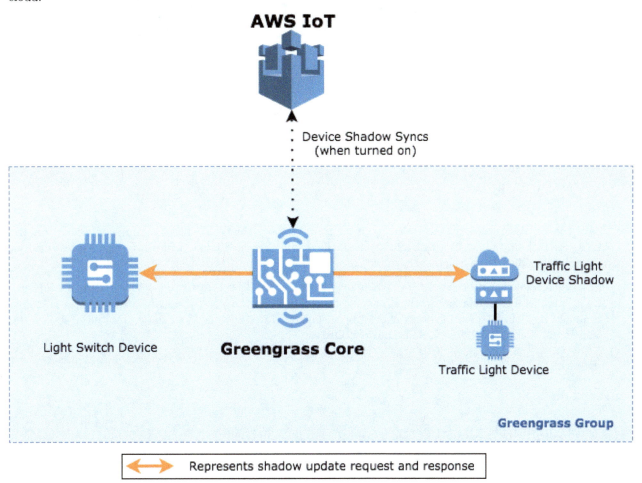

Before you begin, make sure that you have completed Module 1, Module 2, Module 3 (Part 1), and Module 3 (Part 2). You should also understand how to connect devices to an AWS Greengrass core (Module 4). You do not need other components or devices. This module should take about 30 minutes to complete.

Configure Devices and Subscriptions

1. Create two devices in your AWS Greengrass group, **GG_Switch** and **GG_TrafficLight**. Use the default security settings. **Note**
You can detach devices used in earlier modules.

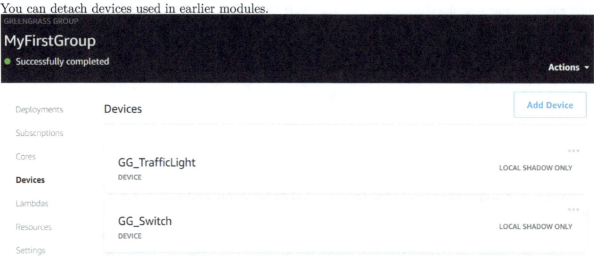

Save the certificates for the devices to your computer – note the GUID-like filename component for the **GG_Switch** and **GG_TrafficLight** devices, these will be needed later. You can reuse the previous root CA from VeriSign or download a new one.

Now, each shadow can be synced to AWS IoT when the AWS Greengrass core is connected to the internet. First, you'll use local shadows without syncing the shadows to the cloud. Later in the module, you enable syncing. By default, cloud syncing should be disabled. If it's not disabled, under **Devices**, choose the ellipsis (…), and then choose **Local Shadow Only**.

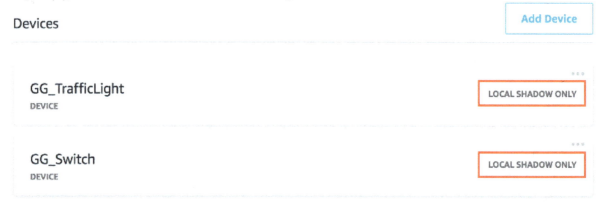

2. Choose **Subscriptions** and create the following subscriptions for your group (For information on the $ sign, see Reserved Topics). For example, to set up the first row subscription, choose **Add Subscription**, for **Select a source** choose **Select**, choose the **Devices** tab, and then choose **GG_Switch**. For **Select a target** choose **Select**, choose **Local Shadow Service**, and then **Next**. For **Optional topic filter**, type (or copy/paste) **$aws/things/GG_TrafficLight/shadow/update**, choose **Next**, and then **Finish**. Using a similar procedure, complete the remaining subscriptions:
[See the AWS documentation website for more details] **Note**
Although you can use wildcards (for example, $aws/things/GG_TrafficLight/shadow/#) to consolidate some of the subscriptions, we do not recommend this practice.

The topic paths must be written exactly as shown in the table. Do not include an extra / at the end of a topic. You can hover your mouse over a **Topic** path to see the full path via tooltip popup:

94

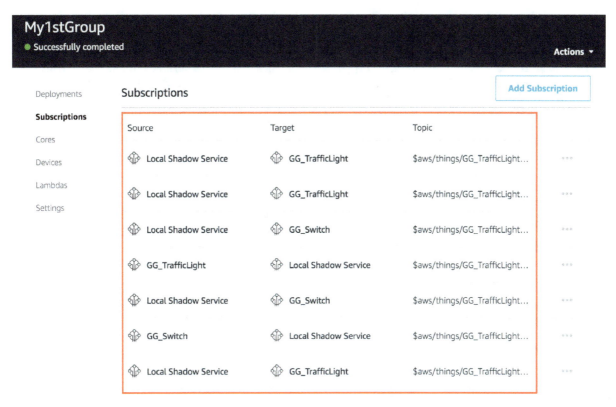

Note

Each device has its own device shadow service. For more information, see Shadow MQTT Topics.

3. Make sure that the AWS Greengrass daemon is running, as described in Deploy Cloud Configurations to a Core Device.

4. On the group configuration page, from the **Actions** menu, choose **Deploy** to deploy the updated group configuration to your AWS Greengrass core device.

Download Required Files

1. If you haven't already done so, install the AWS IoT Device SDK for Python. Follow the instructions in the README file. This SDK is used by all AWS IoT devices to communicate with the AWS IoT cloud and AWS Greengrass cores.

2. From the AWS Greengrass samples repository on GitHub, download the `lightController.py` and `trafficLight.py` files to your computer and move them to the folder containing the GG_Switch and GG_TrafficLight device certificates:

   - 7aa87aa1cf.cert.pem
   - 7aa87aa1cf.private.key
   - 7aa87aa1cf.public.key
   - a27b261ea9.cert.pem
   - a27b261ea9.private.key
   - a27b261ea9.public.key
   - lightController.py
   - root-ca-cert.pem
   - trafficLight.py

   The `lightController.py` script corresponds to the GG_Switch device, and the `trafficLight.py` script corresponds to the GG_TrafficLight device.

Test Communications (Device Syncs Disabled)

1. Open two command-line windows on your computer (not the AWS Greengrass core device). One command-line window is for the GG_Switch device and the other is for the GG_TrafficLight device. Both scripts, when executed for the first time, will run the AWS Greengrass discovery service to connect to the AWS Greengrass core (through the internet). After a device has discovered and successfully connected to the AWS Greengrass core, future operations can be executed locally. Before running the following commands, make sure that your computer and the AWS Greengrass core are connected to the internet using the *same* network.

For the GG_Switch command-line window, run the following:

```
1 cd path-to-certs-folder
2 python lightController.py --endpoint AWS_IOT_ENDPOINT --rootCA root-ca-cert.pem --cert
      switch.cert.pem --key switch.private.key --thingName GG_TrafficLight --clientId
      GG_Switch
```

For the GG_TrafficLight command-line window, run the following:

```
1 cd path-to-certs-folder
2 python trafficLight.py --endpoint AWS_IOT_ENDPOINT --rootCA root-ca-cert.pem --cert light.
      cert.pem --key light.private.key --thingName GG_TrafficLight --clientId GG_TrafficLight
```

Note
To find the endpoint to use for the *AWS_IOT_ENDPOINT* placeholder value, open the AWS IoT console and choose **Settings**.

Every 20 seconds, the switch updates the shadow state to G, Y, and R, and the light displays its new state, as shown next.

GG_Switch output:

GG_TrafficLight output:

1. In the AWS IoT console, choose your AWS Greengrass group, **Devices**, and then **GG_TrafficLight**:

Choose **Shadow**. For **Shadow State**, there should not be any updates to this shadow topic after the GG_Switch changes states because the GG_TrafficLight is set to **LOCAL SHADOW ONLY** as opposed to **SHADOW SYNCING TO CLOUD**, as discussed in the next section.

2. Press Ctrl + C in the GG_Switch (`lightController.py`) command-line window and note that the GG_TrafficLight (`trafficLight.py`) window stops receiving state change messages.

Test Communications (Device Syncs Enabled)

1. In the AWS IoT console, choose your AWS Greengrass group, choose **Devices**, choose the ellipsis for the **GG_TrafficLight** device, then choose **Sync to the Cloud**:

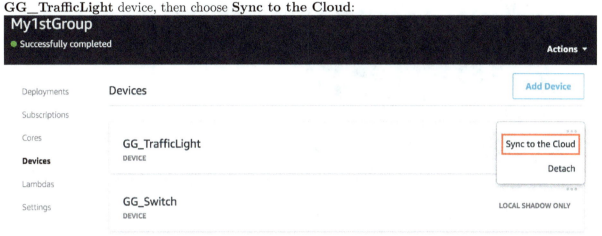

You should receive a notification that the device shadow has been updated.

2. From the **Deployments** page, deploy the updated configuration to your AWS Greengrass core device.

3. Repeat the step in which you create two command-line windows.

4. In the AWS IoT console, choose your AWS Greengrass group, **Devices**, **GG_TrafficLight**, and then **Shadow**.

Because you enabled syncs of the **GG_TrafficLight** shadow to AWS IoT, the shadow state in the cloud should be updated automatically whenever **GG_Switch** sends an update. This functionality can be used to expose the state of an AWS Greengrass device to the AWS IoT cloud.

Shadow Document

Last update: Jan 9, 2018 3:39:53 PM -0800

Shadow state:

```
1 {
2    "desired": {
3       "property": "G"
4    },
5    "reported": {
6       "property": "G"
7    }
8 }
```

Shadow Document

Last update: Jan 9, 2018 3:51:14 PM -0800

Shadow state:

```
1  {
2      "desired": {
3          "property": "Y"
4      },                      After ~20
5      "reported": {          seconds
6          "property": "Y"
7      }
8  }
```

Note

If necessary, you can troubleshoot issues by viewing the AWS Greengrass core logs, particularly `router.log`:

```
1  cd /greengrass/ggc/var/log
2  sudo cat system/router.log | more
```

For more information, see Troubleshooting AWS Greengrass Applications.

Module 6: Accessing AWS Cloud Services

This advanced module shows you how AWS Greengrass cores can interact with other Amazon Web Services in the cloud. It builds on the traffic light example in Module 5 and uses an additional Lambda function that processes shadow states and uploads a summary to an Amazon DynamoDB table.

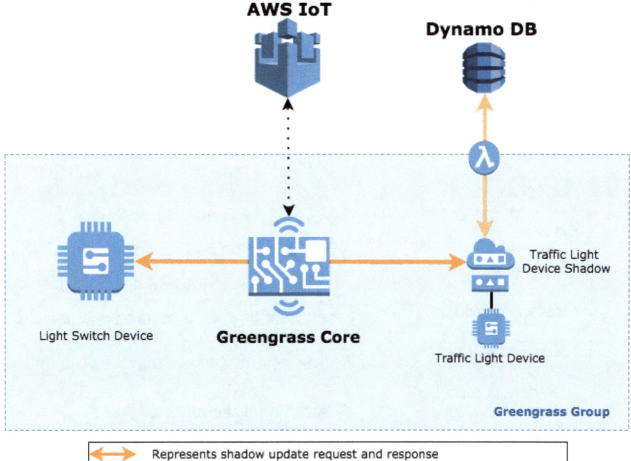

Before you begin, make sure that you have completed Module 1 through Module 5. You do not need other components or devices. This module should take about 30 minutes to complete.

Note
This module creates and updates a table in DynamoDB – most of the operations are small and fall within the AWS Free Tier. See DynamoDB pricing documentation for more information.

Configure IAM Roles

1. Because you are creating a Lambda function that accesses other AWS services, you need to create an IAM role that has access to DynamoDB and AWS Greengrass. For more information about IAM, see the AWS Identity and Access Management documentation.

    In the IAM console, choose **Roles**, and then choose **Create Role**:

    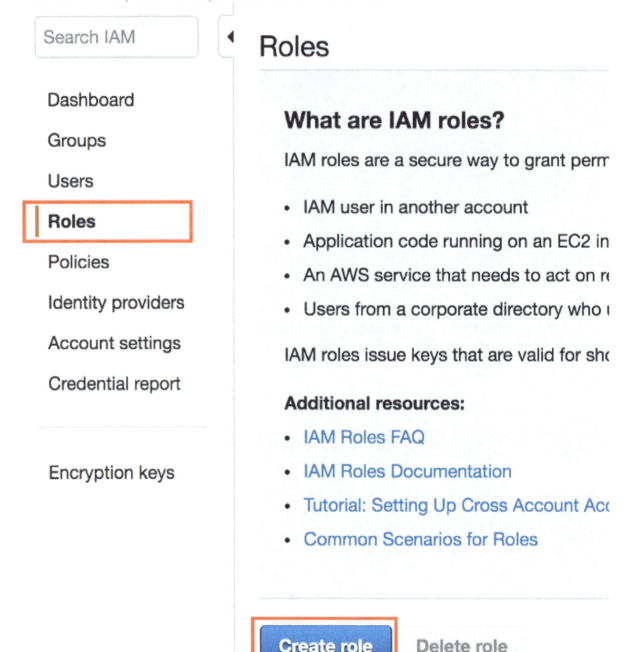

    Choose **AWS service**, and then choose **Greengrass**:

Allows AWS services to perform actions on your behalf. Learn more

Choose the service that will use this role

API Gateway	Data Pipeline	IoT
Auto Scaling	Directory Service	Lambda
Batch	DynamoDB	Lex
CloudFormation	EC2	Machine Learning
CloudHSM	EC2 Container Service	OpsWorks
CloudWatch Events	EMR	RDS
CodeBuild	Elastic Beanstalk	Redshift
CodeDeploy	Elastic Transcoder	S3
Config	Glue	SMS
DMS	Greengrass	SNS

Choose **Next: Permissions**.

On the **Attach permissions policies** page, select the following policies: **AWSGreengrassResourceAccessRolePolicy**, **AWSGreengrassFullAccess**, and **AmazonDynamoDBFullAccess**.

Next, choose **Next: Review**. For **Role name**, type **Greengrass_DynamoDB_Role**, and then choose **Create role**.

Create role

Provide the required information below and review this role before you create it.

Role name* Greengrass_DynamoDB_Role

Maximum 64 characters. Use alphanumeric and '+=,.@-_' characters.

Role description

Maximum 1000 characters. Use alphanumeric and '+=,.@-_' characters.

Trusted entities AWS service: greengrass.amazonaws.com

Policies

AWSGreengrassResourceAccessRolePolicy ↗

AWSGreengrassFullAccess ↗

AmazonDynamoDBFullAccess ↗

* Required   Cancel   Previous   **Create role**

2. Repeat the prior step to create the role for the AWS Lambda service (instead of the AWS Greengrass service). Give the role the same policies (**AWSGreengrassResourceAccessRolePolicy**, **AWSGreengrassFullAccess**, and **AmazonDynamoDBFullAccess**). For **Role name**, type **Lambda_DynamoDB_Role**.

3. In the AWS IoT console, under **Greengrass**, choose **Groups**, and choose your AWS Greengrass group. Choose **Settings**, and then choose **Add Role**:

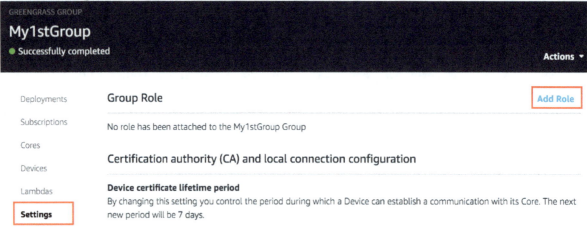

GREENGRASS GROUP
My1stGroup
● Successfully completed   Actions ▾

Deployments   **Group Role**   **Add Role**

Subscriptions   No role has been attached to the My1stGroup Group

Cores

Devices   **Certification authority (CA) and local connection configuration**

Lambdas   **Device certificate lifetime period**
                 By changing this setting you control the period during which a Device can establish a communication with its Core. The next
Settings   new period will be 7 days.

The IAM role you just created should appear in the list. If it does not appear, search for it, select it, and then choose **Save**:

Your Group's IAM Role

Adding an IAM Role to your Group establishes a trust relationship between your trusting account and the Core.

Select an IAM Role with a Greengrass Role Type

🔍 Search Role name
🔘 Greengrass_DynamoDB_Role
⚪ Greengrass_ServiceRole
⚪ TestRole

Back   Save

Create and Configure the Lambda Function

In this step, you create a Lambda function that tracks the number of cars that pass the traffic light. Every time that the `GG_TrafficLight` shadow state changes to `G`, the Lambda simulates the passing of a randomized number of cars (from 1 to 20). On every third `G` light change, the Lambda sends basic statistics, such as min and max, to a DynamoDB table.

1. On your computer, create a folder named `car_aggregator`.

2. From the GitHub repository download the `carAggregator.py` Lambda function to the `car_aggregator` folder.

3. Install the **boto3** package (AWS SDK for Python) and its dependencies in the `car_aggregator` folder by running the following command in a command-line window (for Windows, use an elevated command prompt):

```
1 pip install boto3 -t path-to-car_aggregator-folder
```

This results in a directory listing similar to the following:

car_aggregator
Name
▶ 📁 boto3
▶ 📁 boto3-1.4.7.dist-info
▶ 📁 botocore
▶ 📁 botocore-1.7.43.dist-info
📄 carAggregator.py
▶ 📁 concurrent
▶ 📁 dateutil
▶ 📁 docutils
▶ 📁 docutils-0.14.dist-info
▶ 📁 futures-3.1.1.dist-info
▶ 📁 jmespath
▶ 📁 jmespath-0.9.3.dist-info
▶ 📁 python_dateutil-2.6.1.dist-info
▶ 📁 s3transfer
▶ 📁 s3transfer-0.1.11.dist-info
▶ 📁 six-1.11.0.dist-info
📄 six.py

Greengrass Lambda functions use the AWS SDK to access other Amazon Web Services. For more information, see Boto 3 - The AWS SDK for Python.

4. Compress the contents of the `car_aggregator` folder into a `.zip` file named `car_aggregator.zip`. This is your Lambda function deployment package.

5. In the Lambda console, create a function named **GG_Car_Aggregator**, and set the remaining fields as follows:

   - **Runtime** - choose **Python 2.7**.
   - **Role** - choose **Choose an existing role**.
   - **Existing role** - choose **Lambda_DynamoDB_Role**.

Then, choose **Create function**.

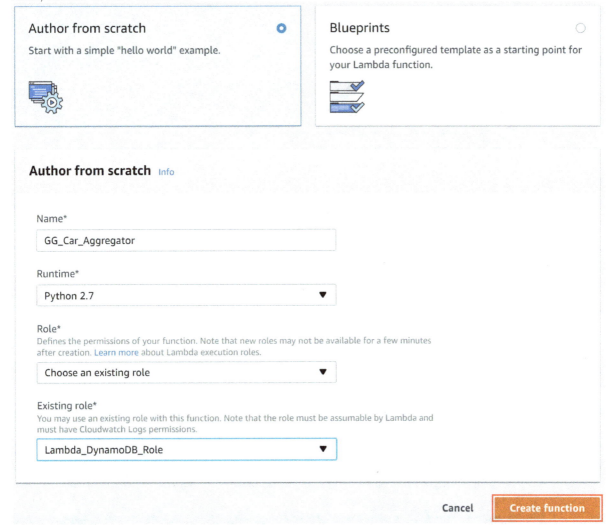

6. Upload your Lambda function deployment package, as follows:

   1. On the **Configuration** tab, under **Function code**, set the following fields:

      - **Code entry type** - choose **Upload a .ZIP file**.
      - **Runtime** - choose **Python 2.7**.
      - **Handler** - type **carAggregator.function_handler**.

   2. Choose **Upload**, and then choose `car_aggregator.zip`.

   3. Choose **Save**.

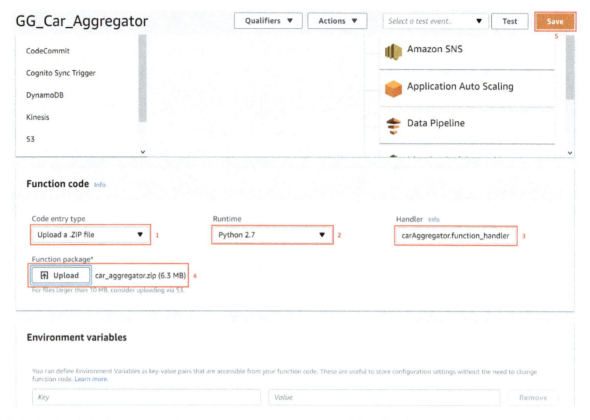

7. Publish the Lambda function, and then create an alias named **GG_CarAggregator**. For step-by-step instructions, see the Publish the Lambda function and Create an alias steps in Module 3 (Part 1).

8. In the AWS IoT console, add the Lambda function that you just created to your AWS Greengrass group, as follows:

   1. On the group configuration page, choose **Lambdas**, and then choose **Add Lambda**:

   2. Choose **Use existing Lambda**:

   Add a Lambda to your Greengrass Group

   Local Lambdas are hosted on your Greengrass Core and connected to each other and devices by Subscriptions, but they can also be deployed individually to your Group.

   Create a new Lambda function

   You will be taken to the AWS Lambda Console and can author a new Lambda function.

   | Create new Lambda |

   Use an existing Lambda function

   You will choose from a list of existing Lambda functions.

   | Use existing Lambda |

   | Back | Use existing Lambda |

   3. Choose **GG_Car_Aggregator**, and then choose **Next**:

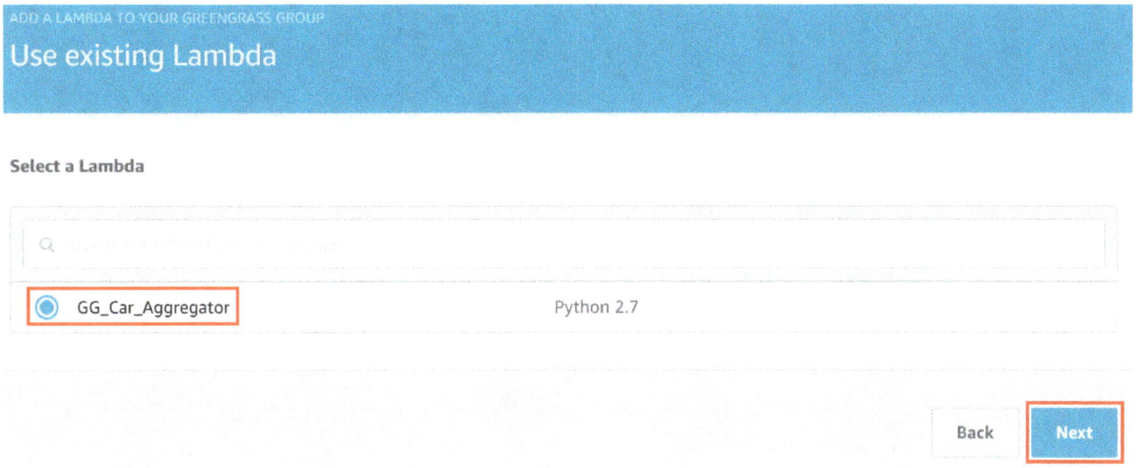
ADD A LAMBDA TO YOUR GREENGRASS GROUP
Use existing Lambda
Select a Lambda
GG_Car_Aggregator
Python 2.7
Back
Next

4. Choose **Alias: GG_CarAggregator**, and then choose **Finish**:

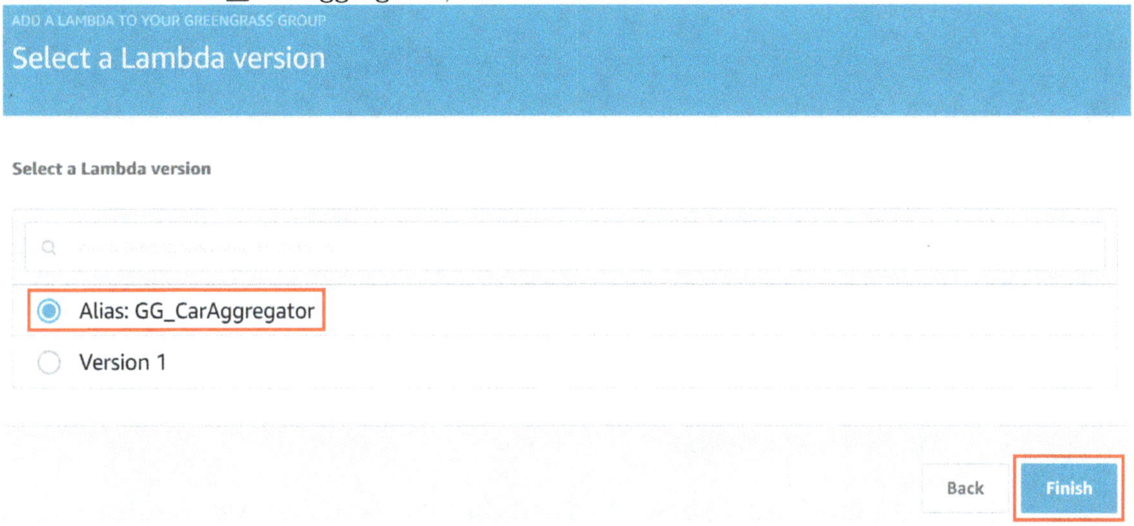
ADD A LAMBDA TO YOUR GREENGRASS GROUP
Select a Lambda version
Select a Lambda version
Alias: GG_CarAggregator
Version 1
Back
Finish

Note

You can remove other Lambda functions from earlier modules.

9. Edit the Lambda function configuration, as follows:

   1. Choose the ellipsis (**...**) associated with the Lambda function, then choose **Edit Configuration**:

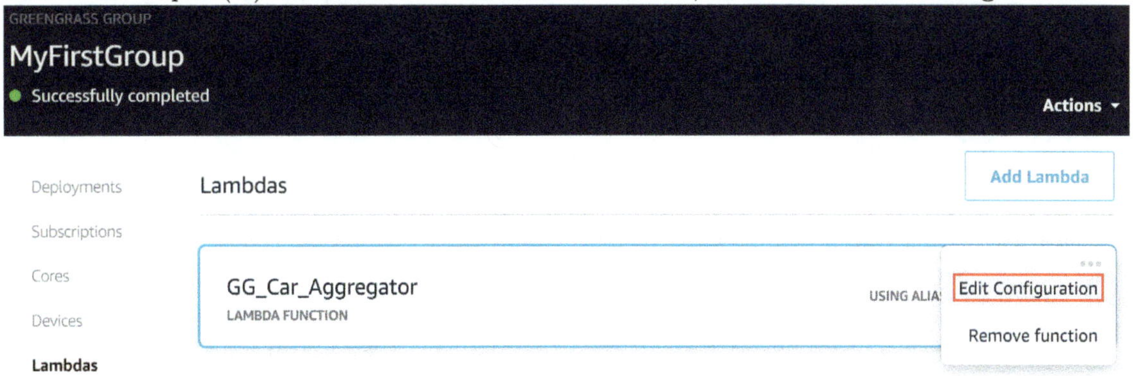
GREENGRASS GROUP
MyFirstGroup
Successfully completed
Actions
Deployments
Subscriptions
Cores
Devices
Lambdas
Lambdas
Add Lambda
GG_Car_Aggregator
LAMBDA FUNCTION
Edit Configuration
Remove function

   2. Under **Lambda lifecycle**, select **Make this function long-lived and keep it running indefinitely**, and then choose **Update**:

Group-specific Lambda configuration

GG_Car_Aggregator

View function in AWS Lambda

Alias GG_CarAggregator

Memory limit

16	⇕	MB	▼

Timeout

3	⇕	Sec...	▼

Lambda lifecycle

◯ **On-demand function**

◉ **Make this function long-lived and keep it running indefinitely**

OTA Updates of AWS Greengrass Core Software

This feature is available for AWS Greengrass Core v1.3.0 and greater.

The AWS Greengrass core software comes packaged with an OTA Update Agent that is capable of updating the core's software or the OTA Update Agent itself to the latest respective versions. You can start an update by invoking the CreateSoftwareUpdateJob API or from the Greengrass console. Updating the Greengrass core software provides the following benefits:

- Fix security vulnerabilities.
- Address software stability issues.
- Deploy new or improved features.

An OTA update makes all these benefits available without having to perform the update manually or having the device which is running the core software physically present. The OTA Update Agent also performs a rollback in case of a failed OTA update. Performing an OTA update is optional but can help you manage your AWS Greengrass core devices. Look for announcements of new versions of the core's software on the Greengrass developer forum.

In order to support an OTA update of Greengrass core software by using the OTA Update Agent, your Greengrass core device must:

- Have available local storage three times the amount of the core's runtime usage requirement.
- Not have trusted boot enabled in the partition containing the Greengrass core platform software. (The AWS Greengrass core can be installed and run on a partition with trusted boot enabled, but cannot perform an OTA update.)
- Have read/write permissions on the partition containing the Greengrass core platform software.
- Have a connection to the AWS cloud.
- Have a correctly configured AWS Greengrass core and appropriate certificates.

Before launching an OTA Update of Greengrass core software, it is important to note the impact that it will have on the devices in your Greengrass group, both on the core device and on client devices connected locally to that core:

- The core will be shut down during the update.
- Any Lambda functions running on the core will be shut down. If those functions write to local resources, they might leave those resources in an incorrect state unless shut down properly.
- During the core's downtime, all its connections with the cloud will be lost and messages routed through the core by client devices will be lost.
- Credential caches will be lost.
- Queues which hold pending work for Lambda functions will be lost.
- Long-lived Lambdas will lose their dynamic state information and all pending work will be dropped.

The following state information will be preserved during an OTA Update:

- Local shadows
- Greengrass logs
- OTA Agent logs

Greengrass OTA Agent

The Greengrass OTA Agent is the software component on the device which handles update jobs created and deployed in the cloud. The Greengrass OTA Agent is distributed in the same software package as the Greengrass core software. The agent is located in `./greengrass/ota/ota_agent/ggc-ota` and creates its logs in `/var/log/greengrass/ota/ggc-ota.txt`.

You can start the Greengrass OTA Agent by executing the binary manually or by integrating it as part of an init script such as a systemd service file. The binary should be run as root. Once started, the Greengrass OTA Agent will begin listening for Greengrass update jobs from the cloud and execute them sequentially. The Greengrass OTA Agent will ignore all other IoT job types.

Do not start multiple OTA Agent instances as this may cause conflicts.

If your Greengrass core or Greengrass OTA Agent is managed by an init system, see Integration With Init Systems for related configurations.

CreateSoftwareUpdateJob API

The CreateSoftwareUpdateJob API creates a software update for a core or for several cores. This API can be used to update the OTA Agent as well as the Greengrass core software. It makes use of the AWS IoT Jobs feature which provides additional commands to manage a Greengrass core software update job. See Jobs for more information on how to manage a Greengrass Update.

The following example shows how to create a Greengrass core software update job using the CLI:

```
1  aws greengrass create-software-update-job \
2      --update-targets-architecture x86_64 \
3      --update-targets arn:aws:iot:us-east-1:123456789012:thing/myDevice \
4      --update-targets-operating-system ubuntu \
5      --software-to-update core \
6      --s3-url-signer-role arn:aws:iam::123456789012:role/IotS3UrlPresigningRole \
7      --update-agent-log-level WARN \
8      --amzn-client-token myClientToken1
```

The create-software-update-job command returns a JSON object containing the job id and job ARN:

```
1  {
2      "IotJobId": "Greengrass-OTA-c3bd7f36-ee80-4d42-8321-a1da0e5b1303",
3      "IotJobArn": "arn:aws:iot:us-east-1:123456789012:job/Greengrass-OTA-c3bd7f36-ee80-4d42-8321-
        a1da0e5b1303"
4  }
```

The create-software-update-job command has the following parameters:

`--update-targets-architecture`
The architecture of the core device. Must be one of **armv7l**, **x86_64** or **aarch64**.

`--update-targets`
A list of the targets to which the OTA update should be applied. The list can contain the ARNS of things which are cores, and the ARNs of thing groups whose members are cores. See IoT thing groups for more information on how to place cores in an IoT thing group.

`--update-targets-operating-system`
The operating system of the core device. Must be one of **ubuntu**, **amazon_linux** or **raspbian**.

`--software-to-update`
Specifies whether the core's software or the OTA Agent software should be updated. Must be one of **core** or **ota_agent**.

`--s3-url-signer-role`
The IAM role which is used to presign the S3 url which links to the Greengrass software update. You must provide a role that has the appropriate policy attached. Here is an example policy document with the minimum required permissions:

```
1  {
2      "Version": "2012-10-17",
3      "Statement": [
4          {
5              "Sid": "AllowsIotToAccessGreengrassOTAUpdateArtifacts",
```

```
 6          "Effect": "Allow",
 7          "Action": [
 8               "s3:GetObject"
 9          ],
10          "Resource": [
11               "arn:aws:s3:::eu-central-1-greengrass-updates/*",
12               "arn:aws:s3:::us-east-1-greengrass-updates/*",
13               "arn:aws:s3:::ap-northeast-1-greengrass-updates/*",
14               "arn:aws:s3:::us-west-2-greengrass-updates/*",
15               "arn:aws:s3:::ap-southeast-2-greengrass-updates/*"
16          ]
17      }
18    ]
19 }
```

Here is an example Assume Role policy document with the minimum required trusted entities:

```
 1 {
 2      "Version": "2012-10-17",
 3      "Statement": [
 4        {
 5             "Action": "sts:AssumeRole",
 6             "Principal": {
 7                  "Service": "iot.amazonaws.com"
 8             },
 9             "Effect": "Allow",
10             "Sid": "AllowIotToAssumeRole"
11        }
12    ]
13 }
```

`--amzn-client-token`
[Optional] A client token used to make idempotent requests. Provide a unique token to prevent duplicate updates from being created due to internal retries.

`--update-agent-log-level`
[Optional] The logging level for log statements generated by the OTA Agent. Must be one of NONE, TRACE, DEBUG, VERBOSE, INFO, WARN, ERROR, or FATAL. The default is ERROR.

Here is an example IAM policy with the minimum permissions required to call the API:

```
 1 {
 2      "Version": "2012-10-17",
 3      "Statement": [
 4        {
 5             "Sid": "AllowCreateSoftwareUpdateJob",
 6             "Action": [
 7                  "greengrass:CreateSoftwareUpdateJob"
 8             ],
 9             "Effect": "Allow",
10             "Resource": "*"
11        },
12        {
13             "Effect": "Allow",
14             "Action": [
15                  "iam:PassRole"
16             ],
```

```
17              "Resource": "arn:aws:s3:us-east-1:123456789012:role/IotS3UrlPresigningRole"
18          },
19          {
20              "Effect": "Allow",
21              "Action": [
22                  "iot:CreateJob"
23              ],
24              "Resource": "*"
25          }
26      ]
27 }
```

Note
Because Greengrass is only supported on a subset of the architecture and operating system combinations possible with this command, `CreateSoftwareUpdateJob` will reject requests except for the following supported platforms: ubuntu/x86_64 ubuntu/aarch64 amazon_linux/x86_64 raspbian/armv7l

Integration with Init systems

During an OTA update, binaries, some of which may be running, will be updated and restarted. This may cause conflicts if an init system is monitoring the state of either the AWS Greengrass core software or the Greengrass OTA Agent during the update. To help integrate the OTA update mechanism with your monitoring strategies, Greengrass provides the opportunity for user-defined shell scripts to run before and after an update. To tell the OTA agent to run these shell scripts, you must include the `managedRespawn = true` flag in the `./greengrass/config/config.json` file. For example:

```
1  {
2
3      "coreThing": {…
4
5      },
6      "runtime": {…
7
8      },
9      "managedRespawn": true
10
11 }
```

When the `managedRespawn` flag is set, the scripts must exist in the directory or the OTA Agent will fail the update. The directory tree should look as follows:

```
1  <greengrass_root>
2  |-- certs
3  |-- config
4  |    |-- config.json
5  |-- ggc
6  |-- usr/scripts
7  |    |-- ggc_pre_update.sh
8  |    |-- ggc_post_update.sh
9  |    |-- ota_pre_update.sh
10 |    |-- ota_post_update.sh
11 |-- ota
```

OTA Self-Update with Managed Respawn

As the OTA Agent prepares to do a self-update, if the `managedRespawn` flag is set to `true` then the OTA Agent will look in the `./greengrass/usr/scripts` directory for the `ota_pre_update.sh` script and run it.

After the OTA Agent completes the update, it will attempt to run the `ota_post_update.sh` script from the `./greengrass/usr/scripts` directory.

AWS Greengrass core Update with Managed Respawn

As the OTA Agent prepares to do an AWS Greengrass core update, if the `managedRespawn` flag is set to `true`, then the OTA Agent will look in the `./greengrass/usr/scripts` directory for the `ggc_pre_update_script.sh` script and run it.

After the OTA Agent completes the update, it will attempt to run the `ggc_post_update.sh` script from the `./greengrass/usr/scripts` directory.

Note:

- The user-defined scripts in `./greengrass/usr/scripts` should be owned by root and executable by root only.
- If `managedRespawn` is set to `true`, the scripts must exist and return a successful return code.
- If `managedRespawn` is set to `false`, the scripts will not be run even if present on the device.
- It is imperative that a device which is the target of an update not run two OTA agents for the same AWS IoT thing. Doing so will cause the two OTA Agents to process the same jobs which will lead to conflicts.

OTA Agent Self-Update

To perform an OTA Agent self-update follow these steps:

1. Ensure that the AWS Greengrass core is correctly provisioned with valid `config.json` file entries and the necessary certificates.

2. If the OTA Agent is being managed by an init system, ensure that `managedRespawn = true` in the `config.json` file and the scripts `ota_pre_update.sh` and `ota_post_update.sh` are present in the `./greengrass/usr/scripts` directory.

3. Start the ggc-ota agent by running `./greengrass/ota/ota_agent/ggc-ota`.

4. Create an OTA self update job in the cloud with the CreateSoftwareUpdateJob API (`aws greengrass create-software-update-job`), making sure the `--software-to-update` parameter is set to `ota_agent`.

5. The OTA Agent will perform a self update.

Greengrass Core Software Update

To perform an AWS Greengrass core software update follow these steps:

1. Ensure that the AWS Greengrass core is correctly provisioned with valid `config.json` file entries and the necessary certificates.

2. If the AWS Greengrass core software is being managed by an init system, ensure that `managedRespawn = true` in the `config.json` file and the scripts `ggc_pre_update.sh` and `ggc_post_update.sh` are present in the `./greengrass/usr/scripts` directory.

3. Start the ggc-ota agent by running `./greengrass/ota/ota_agent/ggc-ota`.

4. Create an OTA self update job in the cloud with the CreateSoftwareUpdateJob API (`aws greengrass create-software-update-job`), making sure the `--software-to-update` parameter is set to `core`.

5. The OTA Agent will perform an update of AWS Greengrass core software.

Reset Deployments

This feature is available for AWS Greengrass Core v1.1.0 and greater.

You may want to reset a group's deployments in order to:

- Delete the group (for example, when the group's core has been reimaged.)
- Move the group's core to a different group.
- Revert the group to its state prior to any deployments.
- Remove the deployment configuration from the core device.
- Delete sensitive data from the core device or from the cloud.
- Deploy a new group configuration to a core without having to replace the core with another in the current group.

Note

The Reset Deployments feature is not available in AWS Greengrass Core Software v1.0.0. Also, note that it's not possible to delete a group that has been deployed using v1.0.0.

The `ResetDeployments` command will clean up all deployment information which is stored in the cloud for a given group. It will then instruct the group's core device to clean up all of its deployment related information as well (Lambda functions, user logs, shadow database and server certificate, but not the user defined config.json or the Greengrass core certificates.) You cannot initiate a reset of deployments for a group if the group currently has a deployment with status `Pending` or `Building`.

```
1  aws greengrass reset-deployments --group-id <GroupId> [--force]
2  ```Arguments for the `reset-deployments` CLI command:
3
4  `--group-id`
5  The group ID\.
6
7  `--force`
8  \[Optional\] Use this parameter if the group's core device has been lost, stolen or destroyed\.
     This option causes the reset deployment process to report success once all deployment
     information in the cloud has been cleaned up, without waiting for a core device to respond\.
      However, if the core device is or becomes active, it will perform its clean up operations
     as well\.
9
10 The output of the `reset-deployments` CLI command will look like this:
```

{ "DeploymentId": "4db95ef8-9309-4774-95a4-eea580b6ceef", "DeploymentArn": "arn:aws:greengrass:us-west-2:106511594199:/greengrass/groups/b744ed45-a7df-4227-860a-8d4492caa412/deployments/4db95ef8-9309-4774-95a4-eea580b6ceef" }

```
1
2  You can check the status of the reset deployment with the `get-deployment-status` CLI command:
```

aws greengrass get-deployment-status --deployment-id DeploymentId --group-id GroupId "'Arguments for the `get-deployment-status` CLI command:

`--deployment-id`
The deployment ID.

`--group-id`
The group ID.

The output of the **get-deployment-status** CLI command will look like this:

```
1  {
2      "DeploymentStatus": "Success",
```

```
3      "UpdatedAt": "2017-04-04T00:00:00.000Z"
4 }
```

The `DeploymentStatus` is set to `Building` when the reset deployment is being prepared. When the reset deployment is ready but the AWS Greengrass core has not picked up the reset deployment, the `DeploymentStatus` is `InProgress`.

Access Local Resources with Lambda Functions

This feature is available for AWS Greengrass Core v1.3.0 and greater.

Developers who use AWS Greengrass can author AWS Lambda functions in the cloud and deploy them to core devices for local execution. On Greengrass cores running Linux, these locally deployed Lambda functions can access local resources that are physically present on the Greengrass core device. For example, to communicate with devices that are connected through Modbus or CANbus, you can enable your Lambda function to access the serial port on the core device. To configure secure access to local resources, you must guarantee the security of your physical hardware and your Greengrass core device OS.

To get started accessing local resources, see the following tutorials:

- How to Configure Local Resource Access Using the AWS Command Line Interface
- How to Configure Local Resource Access Using the AWS Management Console

Supported Resource Types

You can access two types of local resources: volume resources and device resources.

Volume resources
Files or directories on the root file system (except under `/sys`, `/proc`, `/dev`, and `/var`). Only a regular file or directory is allowed for a volume resource.
For example:

- Folders or files used to read or write information across Greengrass Lambda functions (e.g. `/usr/lib/python2.x/site-packages/local`) To configure the `/var`, `/var/run`, and `/var/lib` directories as volume resources, first mount the directory in a different folder and then configure the folder as a volume resource.

Device resources
Files under `/dev`. Only character devices or block devices under `/dev` are allowed for device resources.
For example:

- Serial ports used to communicate with devices connected through serial ports (e.g. `/dev/ttyS0`, `/dev/ttyS1`)
- USB used to connect USB peripherals (e.g. `/dev/ttyUSB0` or `/dev/bus/usb`)
- GPIOs used for sensors and actuators through GPIO (e.g. `/dev/gpiomem`)
- GPUs used to accelerate machine learning using on-board GPUs (e.g. `/dev/nvidia0`)
- Cameras used to capture images and videos (e.g. `/dev/video0`) An exception is `/dev/shm`, which can be configured as a volume resource only. Resources under `/dev/shm` must be granted `rw` permission.

AWS Greengrass also supports resource types that are used to perform machine learning inference. For more information about machine learning resources, see Perform Machine Learning Inference.

Requirements

The following requirements apply to configuring secure access to local resources:

- You must be using AWS Greengrass Core Software v1.3.0 or greater.
- The local resource (including any required drivers and libraries) must be properly installed on the Greengrass core device and consistently available during use.
- The desired operation of the resource, and access to the resource, must not require root privileges.
- Only `read` or `read and write` permissions are available. Lambdas cannot perform privileged operations on the resources.
- You must provide the full path of the local resource on the operating system of the Greengrass core device.
- A resource name or ID has a maximum length of 128 characters and must use the pattern `[a-zA-Z0-9:_-]+`.

Group Owner File Access Permission

An AWS Greengrass Lambda function process normally runs as `ggc_user` and `ggc_group`. However, you can give additional file access permissions to the Lambda function process in the local resource definition, as follows:

- To add the permissions of the Linux group that owns the resource, use the `GroupOwnerSetting#AutoAddGroupOwner` parameter or **Automatically add OS group permissions of the Linux group that owns the resource** console option.
- To add the permissions of a different Linux group, use the `GroupOwnerSetting#GroupOwner` parameter or **Specify another OS group to add permission** console option. The `GroupOwner` value is ignored if `GroupOwnerSetting#AutoAddGroupOwner` is true.

An AWS Greengrass Lambda function process inherits all the file system permissions of `ggc_user`, `ggc_group`, and the Linux group (if added). In order for the Lambda function to access a resource, you need to make sure that the Lambda function process has the required permissions to the resource, using the `chmod(1)` command to change the permission of the resource, if necessary.

See Also

- AWS Greengrass Limits in the *AWS General Reference*

How to Configure Local Resource Access Using the AWS Command Line Interface

This feature is available for AWS Greengrass Core v1.3.0 and greater.

In order to use a local resource, you must add a resource definition to the group definition which will be deployed to your Greengrass core device. The group definition must also contain a Lambda function definition in which you grant access permissions for local resources to your Lambda functions. For more information, including requirements and constraints, see Access Local Resources with Lambda Functions.

This tutorial describes the process of creating a local resource and configuring access to it using the AWS Command Line Interface (CLI). It assumes that you've already created a Greengrass group as described in Getting Started with AWS Greengrass.

For a tutorial that uses the AWS Management Console, see How to Configure Local Resource Access Using the AWS Management Console.

Create Local Resources

First, you create a resource definition that specifies the resources to be accessed by using the command [CreateResourceDefinition](http://docs.aws.amazon.com/greengrass/latest/apireference/createresourcedefinition-post.html). In this example, we create two resources `TestDirectory` and `TestCamera`:

```
1  aws greengrass create-resource-definition  --cli-input-json '{
2      "Name": "MyLocalVolumeResource",
3      "InitialVersion": {
4          "Resources": [
5              {
6                  "Id": "data-volume",
7                  "Name": "TestDirectory",
8                  "ResourceDataContainer": {
9                      "LocalVolumeResourceData": {
10                         "SourcePath": "/src/LRAtest",
11                         "DestinationPath": "/dest/LRAtest",
12                         "GroupOwnerSetting": {
13                             "AutoAddGroupOwner": true,
14                             "GroupOwner": ""
15                         }
16                     }
17                 }
18             },
19             {
20                 "Id": "data-device",
21                 "Name": "TestCamera",
22                 "ResourceDataContainer": {
23                     "LocalDeviceResourceData": {
24                         "SourcePath": "/dev/video0",
25                         "GroupOwnerSetting": {
26                             "AutoAddGroupOwner": true,
27                             "GroupOwner": ""
28                         }
29                     }
30                 }
31             }
```

```
32          ]
33      }
34 }'
```

Resources: A list of `Resource` objects in the Greengrass group. One Greengrass group can have up to 50 resources.

Resource#Id: The unique identifier of the resource. The id is used to refer a resource in the Lambda function configuration. Max length 128 characters. Pattern: [a-zA-Z0-9:_-]+.

Resource#Name: The name of the resource. The resource name is displayed on the Greengrass console. Max length 128 characters. Pattern: [a-zA-Z0-9:_-]+.

LocalVolumeResourceData#SourcePath: The local absolute path of the volume resource on the Greengrass core device. The source path for a volume resource type cannot start with /proc or /sys.

LocalDeviceResourceData#SourcePath: The local absolute path of the device resource. The source path for a device resource can only refer to a character device or block device under /dev.

LocalVolumeResourceData#DestinationPath: The absolute path of the volume resource inside the Lambda environment.

GroupOwnerSetting: Allows you to configure additional group privileges for the Lambda process. This field is optional. For more information, see Group Owner File Access Permission.

GroupOwnerSetting#AutoAddGroupOwner: If true, Greengrass automatically adds the specified Linux OS group owner of the resource to the Lambda process privileges. Thus the Lambda process will have the file access permissions of the added Linux group.

GroupOwnerSetting#GroupOwner: Specifies the name of the Linux OS group whose privileges will be added to the Lambda process. This field is optional.

A resource definition version ARN will be returned by [CreateResourceDefinition](http://docs.aws.amazon.com/greengrass/latest/apireference/createresourcedefinition-post.html) and should be used when updating a group definition. For example:

```
1 {
2     "LatestVersionArn": "arn:aws:greengrass:us-west-2:012345678901:/greengrass/definition/
          resources/ab14d0b5-116e-4951-a322-9cde24a30373/versions/a4d9b882-d025-4760-9cfe-9
          d4fada5390d",
3     "Name": "MyLocalVolumeResource",
4     "LastUpdatedTimestamp": "2017-11-15T01:18:42.153Z",
5     "LatestVersion": "a4d9b882-d025-4760-9cfe-9d4fada5390d",
6     "CreationTimestamp": "2017-11-15T01:18:42.153Z",
7     "Id": "ab14d0b5-116e-4951-a322-9cde24a30373",
8     "Arn": "arn:aws:greengrass:us-west-2:123456789012:/greengrass/definition/resources/ab14d0b5
          -116e-4951-a322-9cde24a30373"
9 }
```

Create the Greengrass Function

After the resources are created, create the Greengrass function using [CreateFunctionDefinition](http://docs.aws.amazon.com/greengrass/latest/apireference/createfunctiondefinition-post.html) and grant the function access to the resource:

```
1
2 aws greengrass create-function-definition --cli-input-json '{
3     "Name": "MyFunctionDefinition",
4     "InitialVersion": {
```

```
 5          "Functions": [
 6              {
 7                  "Id": "greengrassLraTest",
 8                  "FunctionArn": "arn:aws:lambda:us-west-2:012345678901:function:lraTest:1",
 9                  "FunctionConfiguration": {
10                      "Pinned": false,
11                      "MemorySize": 16384,
12                      "Timeout": 30,
13                      "Environment": {
14                          "ResourceAccessPolicies": [
15                              {
16                                  "ResourceId": "data-volume",
17                                  "Permission": "rw"
18                              },
19                              {
20                                  "ResourceId": "data-device",
21                                  "Permission": "ro"
22                              }
23                          ],
24                          "AccessSysfs": true
25                      }
26                  }
27              }
28          ]
29      }
30 }'
```

ResourceAccessPolicies: Contains the `resourceId` and `permission` which grant the Lambda access to the resource. A Lambda function can have at most 10 resources.

ResourceAccessPolicy#Permission: Specifies which permissions the Lambda has on the resource. The available options are `rw` (read/write) or `ro` (readonly).

AccessSysfs: If true, the Lambda process can have read access to the `/sys` folder on the Greengrass core device. This is used in cases where the Greengrass Lambda needs to read device information from `/sys`.

Again, a function definition version ARN is returned by [CreateFunctionDefinition](http://docs.aws.amazon.com/greengrass/latest/apireference/createfunctiondefinition-post.html) and should be used in your group definition version.

```
1 {
2     "LatestVersionArn": "arn:aws:greengrass:us-west-2:012345678901:/greengrass/definition/
          functions/3c9b1685-634f-4592-8dfd-7ae1183c28ad/versions/37f0d50e-ef50-4faf-b125-
          ade8ed12336e",
3     "Name": "MyFunctionDefinition",
4     "LastUpdatedTimestamp": "2017-11-22T02:28:02.325Z",
5     "LatestVersion": "37f0d50e-ef50-4faf-b125-ade8ed12336e",
6     "CreationTimestamp": "2017-11-22T02:28:02.325Z",
7     "Id": "3c9b1685-634f-4592-8dfd-7ae1183c28ad",
8     "Arn": "arn:aws:greengrass:us-west-2:123456789012:/greengrass/definition/functions/3c9b1685
          -634f-4592-8dfd-7ae1183c28ad"
9 }
```

Add the Lambda Function to the Group

Finally, use [CreateGroupVersion](http://docs.aws.amazon.com/greengrass/latest/apireference/creategroupversion-post.html) to add the function to the group. For example:

```
1 aws greengrass create-group-version --group-id "b36a3aeb-3243-47ff-9fa4-7e8d98cd3cf5" \
2 --resource-definition-version-arn "arn:aws:greengrass:us-west-2:123456789012:/greengrass/
      definition/resources/db6bf40b-29d3-4c4e-9574-21ab7d74316c/versions/31d0010f-e19a-4c4c
      -8098-68b79906fb87" \
3 --core-definition-version-arn "arn:aws:greengrass:us-west-2:123456789012:/greengrass/definition/
      cores/adbf3475-f6f3-48e1-84d6-502f02729067/versions/297c419a-9deb-46dd-8ccc-341fc670138b" \
4 --function-definition-version-arn "arn:aws:greengrass:us-west-2:123456789012:/greengrass/
      definition/functions/d1123830-da38-4c4c-a4b7-e92eec7b6d3e/versions/a2e90400-caae-4ffd-b23a-
      db1892a33c78" \
5 --subscription-definition-version-arn "arn:aws:greengrass:us-west-2:123456789012:/greengrass/
      definition/subscriptions/7a8ef3d8-1de3-426c-9554-5b55a32fbcb6/versions/470c858c-7eb3-4abd-9
      d48-230236bfbf6a"
```

A new group version is returned:

```
1 {
2     "Arn": "arn:aws:greengrass:us-west-2:012345678901:/greengrass/groups/b36a3aeb-3243-47ff-9fa4
          -7e8d98cd3cf5/versions/291917fb-ec54-4895-823e-27b52da25481",
3     "Version": "291917fb-ec54-4895-823e-27b52da25481",
4     "CreationTimestamp": "2017-11-22T01:47:22.487Z",
5     "Id": "b36a3aeb-3243-47ff-9fa4-7e8d98cd3cf5"
6 }
```

Your Greengrass group now contains the *lraTest* Lambda function that has access to two resources: TestDirectory and TestCamera.

Here is an example Lambda function, `lraTest.py`, written in Python, which writes to the local volume resource:

```
 1 # lraTest.py
 2 # Demonstrates a simple use case of local resource access.
 3 # This Lambda function writes a file "test" to a volume mounted inside
 4 # the Lambda environment under "/dest/LRAtest". Then it reads the file and
 5 # publishes the content to the AWS IoT "LRA/test" topic.
 6
 7 import sys
 8 import greengrasssdk
 9 import platform
10 import os
11 import logging
12
13 # Create a Greengrass Core SDK client.
14 client = greengrasssdk.client('iot-data')
15 volumePath = '/dest/LRAtest'
16
17 def function_handler(event, context):
18     client.publish(topic='LRA/test', payload='Sent from AWS Greengrass Core.')
19     try:
20         volumeInfo = os.stat(volumePath)
21         client.publish(topic='LRA/test', payload=str(volumeInfo))
22         with open(volumePath + '/test', 'a') as output:
23             output.write('Successfully write to a file.\n')
24         with open(volumePath + '/test', 'r') as myfile:
```

```
25          data = myfile.read()
26      client.publish(topic='LRA/test', payload=data)
27  except Exception as e:
28      logging.error("Experiencing error :{}".format(e))
29  return
```

These commands are provided by the Greengrass API to create and manage resource definitions and resource definition versions:

- CreateResourceDefinition
- CreateResourceDefinitionVersion
- DeleteResourceDefinition
- GetResourceDefinition
- GetResourceDefinitionVersion
- ListResourceDefinitions
- ListResourceDefinitionVersions
- UpdateResourceDefinition

Troubleshooting

- **Q:** Why does my Greengrass group deployment fail with an error similar to:

```
1 group config is invalid:
2     ggc_user or [ggc_group root tty] don't have ro permission on the file: /dev/tty0
```

A: This error indicates that the Lambda process doesn't have permission to access the specified resource. The solution is to change the file permission of the resource so that Lambda can access it (see Group Owner File Access Permission for more details).

- **Q:** When I configure /var/run as a volume resource, why does the Lambda function fail to start with an error message in the runtime.log:

```
1 [ERROR]-container_process.go:39,Runtime execution error: unable to start lambda container.
2 container_linux.go:259: starting container process caused "process_linux.go:345:
3 container init caused \"rootfs_linux.go:62: mounting \\\"/var/run\\\" to rootfs \\\"/
    greengrass/ggc/packages/1.3.0/rootfs_sys\\\" at \\\"/greengrass/ggc/packages/1.3.0/
    rootfs_sys/run\\\"
4 caused \\\"invalid argument\\\"\""
```

A: AWS Greengrass core currently doesn't support the configuration of /var, /var/run, and /var/lib as volume resources. One workaround is to first mount /var, /var/run or /var/lib in a different folder and then configure the folder as a volume resource.

- **Q:** When I configure /dev/shm as a volume resource with readonly permission, why does the Lambda function fail to start with an error in the runtime.log:

```
1 [ERROR]-container_process.go:39,Runtime execution error: unable to start lambda container.
2 container_linux.go:259: starting container process caused "process_linux.go:345:
3 container init caused \"rootfs_linux.go:62: mounting \\\"/dev/shm\\\" to rootfs \\\"/
    greengrass/ggc/packages/1.3.0/rootfs_sys\\\" at \\\"/greengrass/ggc/packages/1.3.0/
    rootfs_sys/dev/shm\\\"
4 caused \\\"operation not permitted"\\\"\""
```

A: /dev/shm can only be configured as read/write. Changing the resource permission to rw will resolve the issue.

How to Configure Local Resource Access Using the AWS Management Console

This feature is available for AWS Greengrass Core v1.3.0 and greater.

You can configure Lambda functions to securely access local resources on the host Greengrass core device. *Local resources* refer to buses and peripherals that are physically on the host, or file system volumes on the host OS. For more information, including requirements and constraints, see Access Local Resources with Lambda Functions.

This tutorial describes how to use the AWS Management Console to configure access to local resources that are present on an AWS Greengrass core device. It contains the following high-level steps:

1. Create a Lambda Function Deployment Package

2. Create and Publish a Lambda Function

3. Add the Lambda Function to the Group

4. Add a Local Resource to the Group

5. Add Subscriptions to the Group

6. Deploy the Group

For a tutorial that uses the AWS Command Line Interface (CLI), see How to Configure Local Resource Access Using the AWS Command Line Interface.

Prerequisites

To complete this tutorial, you need:

- A Greengrass group and a Greengrass core (v1.3.0 or greater). To learn how to create a Greengrass group or core, see Getting Started with AWS Greengrass.

- The following directories created on the Greengrass core device:

  - /src/LRAtest
  - /dest/LRAtest

  The owner group of these directories must have read and write access to the directories. For example, you might use the following command to grant access:

```
1 sudo chmod 0775 /src/LRAtest
```

Step 1: Create a Lambda Function Deployment Package

In this step, you create a Lambda function deployment package, which is a ZIP file that contains the function's code and dependencies. You also download the AWS Greengrass Core SDK to include in the package as a dependency.

1. On your computer, copy the following Python script to a local file named lraTest.py. This is the app logic for the Lambda function.

```
1 # lraTest.py
2 # Demonstrates a simple use case of local resource access.
3 # This Lambda function writes a file "test" to a volume mounted inside
4 # the Lambda environment under "/dest/LRAtest". Then it reads the file and
5 # publishes the content to the AWS IoT "LRA/test" topic.
6
```

```
 7 import sys
 8 import greengrasssdk
 9 import platform
10 import os
11 import logging
12
13 # Create a Greengrass Core SDK client.
14 client = greengrasssdk.client('iot-data')
15 volumePath = '/dest/LRAtest'
16
17 def function_handler(event, context):
18     client.publish(topic='LRA/test', payload='Sent from AWS Greengrass Core.')
19     try:
20         volumeInfo = os.stat(volumePath)
21         client.publish(topic='LRA/test', payload=str(volumeInfo))
22         with open(volumePath + '/test', 'a') as output:
23             output.write('Successfully write to a file.\n')
24         with open(volumePath + '/test', 'r') as myfile:
25             data = myfile.read()
26         client.publish(topic='LRA/test', payload=data)
27     except Exception as e:
28         logging.error("Experiencing error :{}".format(e))
29     return
```

2. Download the AWS Greengrass Core SDK Python 2.7 version 1.1.0, as follows:

   1. In the AWS IoT console, in the left pane, choose **Software**.

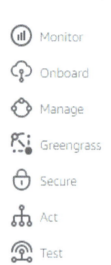

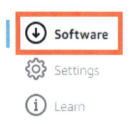

2. Under **SDKs**, for **AWS Greengrass Core SDK**, choose **Configure download**.

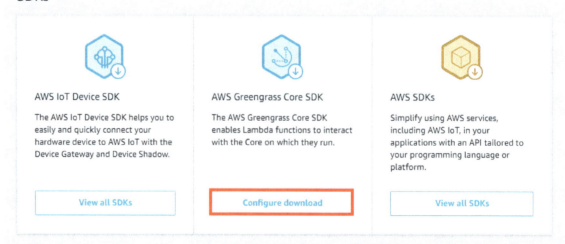

3. Choose **Python 2.7 version 1.1.0**, and then choose **Download Greengrass Core SDK**.

The AWS Greengrass Core SDK enables Lambda functions to interact with the Greengrass Core on which they run. This allows them to publish messages and interact with shadow data or invoke Lambda functions within the Greengrass Core.

Version 1.1.0	greengrass-core-python-sdk-1.1.0.tar.gz

Python 2.7 version 1.1.0 ▼	**Download Greengrass Core SDK**

3. Unpack the `greengrass-core-python-sdk-1.1.0.tar.gz` file. **Note**
   For ways that you can do this on different platforms, see this step in the Getting Started section. For example, you might use the following `tar` command:

```
1  tar -xzf greengrass-core-python-sdk-1.1.0.tar.gz
```

4. Open the extracted aws_greengrass_core_sdk/sdk folder, and unzip `python_sdk_1_1_0.zip`.

5. Zip the following items into a file named `lraTestLambda.zip`:

   - **lraTest.py**. App logic.
   - **greengrasssdk**. Required library for all Python Lambda functions.
   - **Greengrass AWS SW License (IoT additiona) vr6.txt**. Required Greengrass Core Software License Agreement.

   The `lraTestLambda.zip` file is your Lambda function deployment package. Now you're ready to create a Lambda function and upload the deployment package.

Step 2: Create and Publish a Lambda Function

In this step, you use the AWS Lambda console to create a Lambda function and configure it to use your deployment package. Then, you publish a function version and create an alias.

First, create the Lambda function.

1. In the AWS Management Console, choose **Services**, and open the AWS Lambda console.

AWS services

```
Lambda

Lambda
Run Code without Thinking about Servers

Amazon Lex
Build Voice and Text Chatbots
```

2. Choose **Create function**.

3. Choose **Author from scratch**.

4. In the **Author from scratch** section, use the following values:
   [See the AWS documentation website for more details]

5. At the bottom of the page, choose **Create function**.

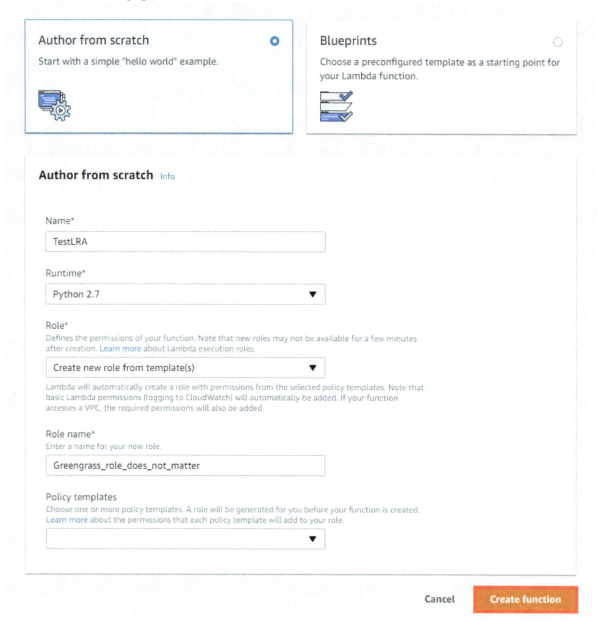

Now, upload your Lambda function deployment package and register the handler.

1. On the **Configuration** tab for the TestLRA function, in **Function code**, use the following values: [See the AWS documentation website for more details]

2. Choose **Upload**.

3. Choose your `lraTestLambda.zip` deployment package.

4. At the top of the page, choose **Save**.

Tip
You can see your code in the **Function code** section by choosing **Edit code inline** from the **Code entry type** menu.

Next, publish the first version of your Lambda function. Then, create an alias for the version.

Note
Greengrass groups can reference a Lambda function by alias (recommended) or by version. Using an alias makes it easier to manage code updates because you don't have to change your subscription table or group definition when the function code is updated. Instead, you just point the alias to the new function version.

1. From the **Actions** menu, choose **Publish new version**.

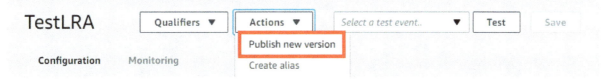

2. For **Version description**, type **First version**, and then choose **Publish**.

3. On the **TestLRA: 1** configuration page, from the **Actions** menu, choose **Create alias**.

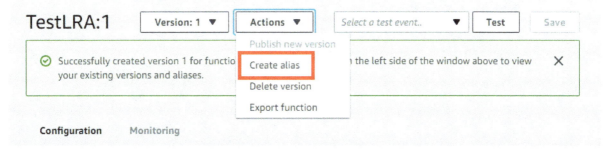

4. On the **Create a new alias** page, use the following values:
   [See the AWS documentation website for more details] **Note**
   AWS Greengrass doesn't support Lambda aliases for **$LATEST** versions.

5. Choose **Create**.

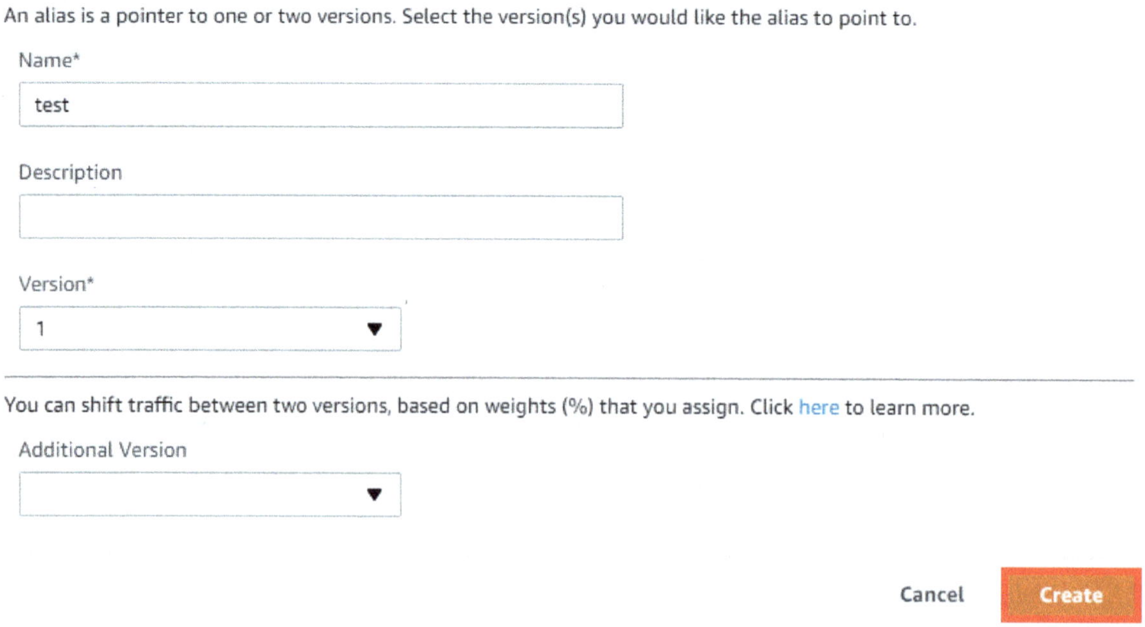

An alias is a pointer to one or two versions. Select the version(s) you would like the alias to point to.

Name*

```
test
```

Description

```

```

Version*

```
1                                    ▼
```

You can shift traffic between two versions, based on weights (%) that you assign. Click here to learn more.

Additional Version

```
                                     ▼
```

Cancel   **Create**

You can now add the Lambda function to your Greengrass group.

Step 3: Add the Lambda Function to the Greengrass Group

In this step, you add the TestLRA function to your group and configure the function's lifecycle. First, add the Lambda function to your Greengrass group.

1. In the AWS IoT console, choose **Greengrass**, and then choose **Groups**.

2. Choose the Greengrass group where you want to add the Lambda function.

3. On the group configuration page, choose **Lambdas**, and then choose **Add Lambda**.

4. On the **Add a Lambda to your Greengrass Group** page, choose **Use existing Lambda**.

5. On the **Use existing Lambda** page, choose **TestLRA**, and then choose **Next**.

6. On the **Select a Lambda version** page, choose **Alias:test**, and then choose **Finish**.

Next, configure the lifecycle of the Lambda function.

1. On the **Lambdas** page, choose the TestLRA Lambda function.

2. On the **TestLRA** configuration page, choose **Edit**.

3. On the **Group-specific Lambda configuration** page, use the following values:
   [See the AWS documentation website for more details] **Note**
   A *long-lived*—or *pinned*—Lambda function starts automatically after AWS Greengrass starts and keeps running in its own container (or sandbox). This is in contrast to an *on-demand* Lambda function, which starts only when invoked and stops when there are no tasks left to execute. When possible, you should use on-demand Lambda functions because they are less resource intensive than long-lived functions. However, the Lambda in this tutorial requires a long-lived lifecycle.

4. At the bottom of the page, choose **Update**.

Step 4: Add a Local Resource to the Greengrass Group

In this step, you add a local volume resource to a Greengrass group and grant the function read and write access to the resource. A local resource has a group-level scope, which makes it accessible by all Lambda functions in the group.

1. On the group configuration page, choose **Resources**.

Deployments

Subscriptions

Cores

Devices

Lambdas

Resources

Settings

2. For **Local resources**, choose **Add**.

3. On the **Create a local resource** page, use the following values:
[See the AWS documentation website for more details]

   The **Source path** is the local absolute path of the resource on the file system of the core device. This path can't start with /proc or /sys.

   The **Destination path** is the absolute path of the resource in the Lambda namespace.

   The **Group owner file access permission** option lets you grant additional file access permissions to the Lambda process. For more information, see Group Owner File Access Permission.

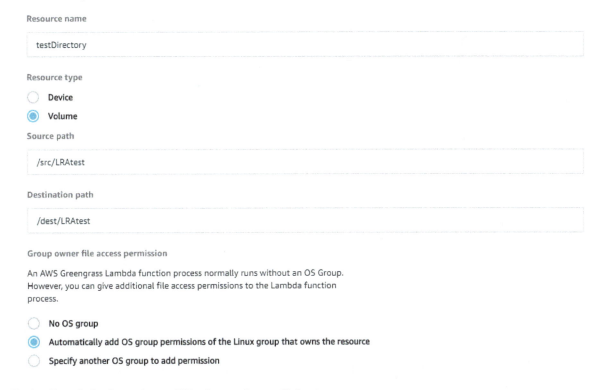

Resource name

testDirectory

Resource type

○ Device

● Volume

Source path

/src/LRAtest

Destination path

/dest/LRAtest

Group owner file access permission

An AWS Greengrass Lambda function process normally runs without an OS Group. However, you can give additional file access permissions to the Lambda function process.

○ No OS group

● Automatically add OS group permissions of the Linux group that owns the resource

○ Specify another OS group to add permission

4. Under **Lambda function affiliations**, choose **Select**.

5. Choose **TestLRA**, choose **Read and write access**, and then choose **Done**.

6. At the bottom of the page, choose **Save**. The **Resources** page displays the new testDirectory resource.

Step 5: Add Subscriptions to the Greengrass Group

In this step, you add two subscriptions to the Greengrass group. These subscriptions enable bidirectional communication between the Lambda function and AWS IoT.

First, create a subscription for the Lambda function to send messages to AWS Greengrass.

1. On the group configuration page, choose **Subscriptions**, and then choose **Add Subscription**.

2. On the **Select your source and target** page, configure the source and target, as follows:

    1. For **Select a source**, choose **Lambdas**, and then choose **TestLRA**.

    2. For **Select a target**, choose **Services**, and then choose **IoT Cloud**.

    3. Choose **Next**.

3. On the **Filter your data with a topic** page, for **Optional topic filter**, type **LRA/test**, and then choose **Next**.

4. Choose **Finish**. The **Subscriptions** page displays the new subscription.

Next, configure a subscription that invokes the function from AWS IoT.

1. On the **Subscriptions** page, choose **Add Subscription**.

2. On the **Select your source and target** page, configure the source and target, as follows:

   1. For **Select a source**, choose **Services**, and then choose **IoT Cloud**.

   2. For **Select a target**, choose **Lambdas**, and then choose **TestLRA**.

   3. Choose **Next**.

3. On the **Filter your data with a topic** page, for **Optional topic filter**, type **invoke/LRAFunction**, and then choose **Next**.

4. Choose **Finish**. The **Subscriptions** page displays both subscriptions.

Step 6: Deploy the AWS Greengrass Group

In this step, you deploy the current version of the group definition.

1. Make sure that the AWS Greengrass core is running. Run the following commands in your Raspberry Pi terminal, as needed.

    1. To check whether the daemon is running:

    ```
    1 ps aux | grep -E 'greengrass.*daemon'
    ```

    If the output contains a `root` entry for `/greengrass/ggc/packages/1.5.0/bin/daemon`, then the daemon is running. **Note**
    The version in the path depends on the AWS Greengrass Core software version that's installed on your core device.

    2. To start the daemon:

    ```
    1 cd /greengrass/ggc/core/
    2 sudo ./greengrassd start
    ```

2. On the group configuration page, choose **Deployments**, and from the **Actions** menu, choose **Deploy**.

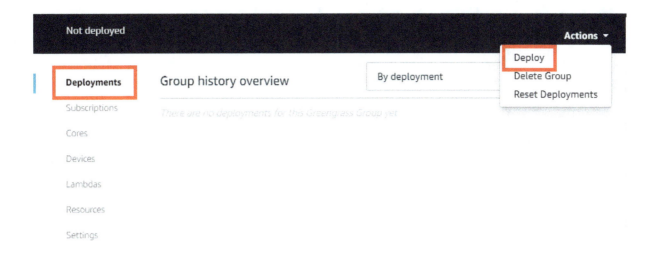

3. On the **Configure how devices discover your core** page, choose **Automatic detection**.

This enables devices to automatically acquire connectivity information for the core, such as IP address, DNS, and port number. Automatic detection is recommended, but AWS Greengrass also supports manually specified endpoints. You're only prompted for the discovery method the first time that the group is deployed.

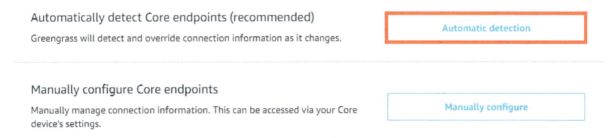

Note

If prompted, grant permission to create the AWS Greengrass service role on your behalf, which allows AWS Greengrass to access other AWS services. You need to do this only one time per account.

The **Deployments** page shows the deployment timestamp, version ID, and status. When completed, the deployment should show a **Successfully completed** status.

Test Local Resource Access

Now you can verify whether the local resource access is configured correctly. To test, you subscribe to the **LRA/test** topic and publish to the **invoke/LRAFunction** topic. The test is successful if the Lambda function sends the expected payload to AWS IoT.

1. On the AWS IoT console home page, in the left pane, choose **Test**.

2. In the **Subscriptions** section, use the following values:
   [See the AWS documentation website for more details]

3. Choose **Subscribe to topic**. Your Lambda function publishes to the LRA/test topic.

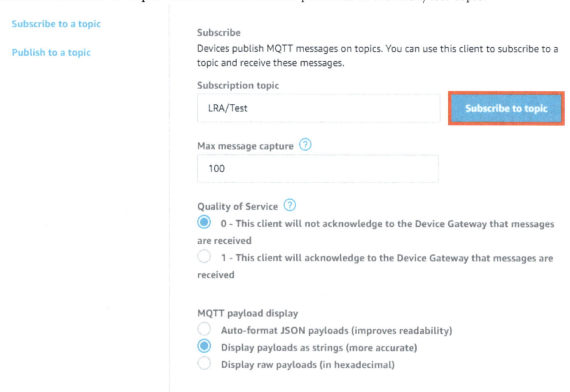

4. In the **Publish** section, type **invoke/LRAFunction**, and then choose **Publish to topic** to invoke your Lambda function. The test is successful if the page displays the function's three message payloads.

You can see the test file that the Lambda creates by looking in the /src/LRAtest directory on the Greengrass core device. Although the Lambda writes to a file in the /dest/LRAtest directory, that file is visible in the Lambda namespace only—you cant' see it in a regular Linux namespace. However, any changes to the destination path are reflected in the source path on the actual file system.

For help troubleshooting any issues that you encounter, see Troubleshooting AWS Greengrass Applications.

Perform Machine Learning Inference

This feature is available for AWS Greengrass Core v1.5.0 only.

With AWS Greengrass, you can perform machine learning (ML) inference at the edge on locally generated data using cloud-trained models. This lets you benefit from the low latency and cost savings of running local inference, yet still take advantage of cloud computing power for training models and complex processing.

To get started performing local inference, see How to Configure Machine Learning Inference Using the AWS Management Console.

How AWS Greengrass ML Inference Works

You can train your inference models anywhere, deploy them locally as *machine learning resources* in a Greengrass group, and then access them from Greengrass Lambda functions. For example, you can build and train deep-learning models in Amazon SageMaker and deploy them to your Greengrass core. Then, your Lambda functions can use the local models to perform inference on connected devices and send new training data back to the cloud.

The following diagram shows the AWS Greengrass ML inference workflow.

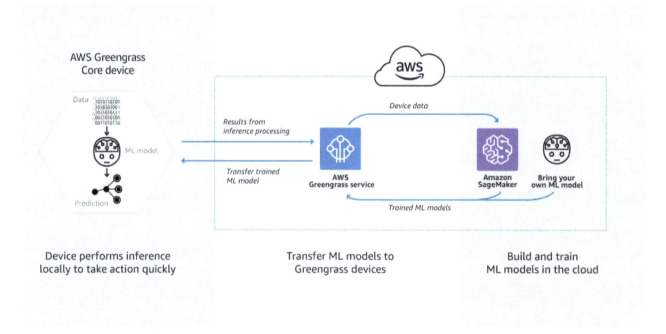

AWS Greengrass ML inference simplifies each step of the ML workflow, including:

- Building and deploying ML framework prototypes.
- Accessing cloud-trained models and deploying them to Greengrass core devices.
- Creating inference apps that can access hardware accelerators (such as GPUs and FPGAs) as local resources.

Machine Learning Resources

Machine learning resources represent cloud-trained inference models that are deployed to an AWS Greengrass core. To deploy machine learning resources, first you add the resources to a Greengrass group, and then you define how Lambda functions in the group can access them. During group deployment, AWS Greengrass retrieves the source model packages from the cloud and extracts them to directories inside the Lambda runtime namespace. Then, Greengrass Lambda functions use the locally deployed models to perform inference.

To update a locally deployed model, first update the source model (in the cloud) that corresponds to the machine learning resource, and then deploy the group. During deployment, AWS Greengrass checks the source for changes. If changes are detected, then AWS Greengrass updates the local model.

Supported Model Sources

AWS Greengrass supports Amazon SageMaker and Amazon S3 model sources for machine learning resources.

The following requirements apply to model sources:

- S3 buckets that store your Amazon SageMaker and Amazon S3 model sources must not be encrypted using SSE-C. For buckets that use server-side encryption, AWS Greengrass ML inference currently supports only SSE-S3 or SSE-KMS encryption options. For more information about server-side encryption options, see Protecting Data Using Server-Side Encryption in the * Amazon Simple Storage Service Developer Guide*.
- The names of S3 buckets that store your Amazon SageMaker and Amazon S3 model sources must not include periods ("."). For more information, see the rule about using virtual hosted–style buckets with SSL in Rules for Bucket Naming in the * Amazon Simple Storage Service Developer Guide*.
- Service-level region support must be available, as follows:
  - Amazon SageMaker model sources are supported only in regions that have both AWS Greengrass support and Amazon SageMaker support.
  - Amazon S3 model sources are supported only in regions that have both AWS Greengrass support and Amazon S3 support.
- AWS Greengrass must have **read** permission to the model source, as described in the following sections.

Amazon SageMaker
AWS Greengrass supports models that are saved as Amazon SageMaker training jobs.
If you configured your Amazon SageMaker environment by creating a bucket whose name contains `sagemaker`, then AWS Greengrass has sufficient permission to access your Amazon SageMaker training jobs. The AWSGreengrassResourceAccessRolePolicy managed policy allows access to buckets whose name contains the string `sagemaker`. This policy is attached to the Greengrass service role.
Otherwise, you must grant AWS Greengrass **read** permission to the bucket where your training job is stored. To do this, embed the following inline policy in the Greengrass service role. You can list multiple bucket ARNs.

```
1  {
2      "Version": "2012-10-17",
3      "Statement": [
4          {
5              "Effect": "Allow",
6              "Action": [
7                  "s3:GetObject"
8              ],
9              "Resource": [
10                  "arn:aws:s3:::my-bucket-name"
11              ]
12          }
13      ]
14  }
```

Amazon SageMaker is a fully managed ML service that enables you to build and train models using built-in or custom algorithms. For more information, see What Is Amazon SageMaker in the *Amazon SageMaker Developer Guide.*

Amazon S3
AWS Greengrass supports models that are stored in Amazon S3 as `tar.gz` or `.zip` files.
To enable AWS Greengrass to access models that are stored in Amazon S3 buckets, you must grant AWS Greengrass **read** permission to access the buckets by doing **one** of the following:

- Store your model in a bucket whose name contains **greengrass**.

  The AWSGreengrassResourceAccessRolePolicy managed policy allows access to buckets whose name contains the string **greengrass**. This policy is attached to the Greengrass service role.

- Embed an inline policy in the Greengrass service role.

  If your bucket name doesn't contain **greengrass**, add the following inline policy to the service role. You can list multiple bucket ARNs.

```
{
    "Version": "2012-10-17",
    "Statement": [
        {
            "Effect": "Allow",
            "Action": [
                "s3:GetObject"
            ],
            "Resource": [
                "arn:aws:s3:::my-bucket-name"
            ]
        }
    ]
}
```

  For more information, see Embedding Inline Policies in the *IAM User Guide*.

Requirements

The following requirements apply for creating and using machine learning resources:

- You must be using AWS Greengrass Core Software v1.5.0.
- Access to the local destination directory where the resource is stored must not require root privileges.
- Lambda functions can't perform privileged operations on the resource. Only **read** or **read and write** permissions are available.
- You must provide the full path of the resource on the operating system of the core device.
- A resource name or ID has a maximum length of 128 characters and must use the pattern [a-zA-Z0-9:_-]+.

Precompiled Libraries for ML Frameworks

To help you quickly get started experimenting with ML inference, AWS Greengrass provides precompiled libraries for the following ML frameworks under the Apache License 2.0:

- Apache MXNet
- TensorFlow

The precompiled MXNet and TensorFlow libraries can be installed on NVIDIA Jetson TX2, Intel Atom, and Raspberry Pi platforms. The libraries are available from the **Software** page of the AWS IoT console. You can install them directly on your core or include them as part of the software in your Greengrass group.

Be sure to read the following information about compatibility and limitations.

MXNet Versioning

Apache MXNet doesn't currently ensure forward compatibility, so models that you train using later versions of the framework might not work properly in earlier versions of the framework. To avoid conflicts between the model-training and model-serving stages, and to provide a consistent end-to-end experience, use the same MXNet framework version in both stages.

Note
We recommend using MXNet v0.11 for AWS Greengrass ML inference. To configure Amazon SageMaker to train models using the recommended version, see How to Configure Amazon SageMaker to Use MXNet v0.11.

TensorFlow Model-Serving Limitations on Raspberry Pi

TensorFlow officially only supports installation on 64-bit laptop or desktop operating systems. Therefore, the precompiled TensorFlow libraries that AWS Greengrass provides for 32-bit ARM platforms (such as Raspberry Pi) have inherent limitations and are intended for experimentation purposes only.

The following recommendations for improving inference results are based on our tests with the 32-bit ARM precompiled libraries on the Raspberry Pi platform. These recommendations are intended for advanced users for reference only, without guarantees of any kind.

- Models that are trained using the Checkpoint format should be "frozen" to the protocol buffer format before serving. For an example, see the TensorFlow-Slim image classification model library.

- Don't use the TF-Estimator and TF-Slim libraries in either training or inference code. Instead, use the .pb file model-loading pattern that's shown in the following example.

```
1 graph = tf.Graph()
2 graph_def = tf.GraphDef()
3 graph_def.ParseFromString(pb_file.read())
4 with graph.as_default():
5   tf.import_graph_def(graph_def)
```

Note
For more information about supported platforms for TensorFlow, see Installing TensorFlow in the TensorFlow documentation.

How to Configure Amazon SageMaker to Use MXNet v0.11

This section describes how to configure Amazon SageMaker to train models using MXNet v0.11. This is the recommended version for AWS Greengrass ML inference.

1. Create an Amazon S3 bucket by following the Create a Bucket procedure in the *Amazon Simple Storage Service Console User Guide.*

   Make sure that you include **sagemaker** in the name (for example, **sagemaker-*datetime***).

2. Create an Amazon SageMaker notebook instance by following the Create an Amazon SageMaker Notebook Instance procedure in the *Amazon SageMaker Developer Guide.*

3. When the status of the notebook instance is **InService**, choose the **Open** action for your notebook instance.

4. Choose **New**, and then choose **conda_mxnet_p27** from the list of Jupyter kernels. This opens an MXNet environment for Python 2.7.

5. Override the default **sagemaker.mxnet.MXNet.train_image** field in the code with an MXNet v0.11 container image, as follows:

1. In the following code, replace the *container-image* placeholder value with the MXNet v0.11 container image that you want to use:

   - For MXNet v0.11 on Python2.7 with CPU, specify **sagemaker-mxnet-py2-cpu**.
   - For MXNet v0.11 on Python2.7 with GPU, specify **sagemaker-mxnet-py2-gpu**.
   - For MXNet v0.11 on Python 3.6 with CPU, specify **sagemaker-mxnet-py3-cpu**.
   - For MXNet v0.11 on Python 3.6 with GPU, specify **sagemaker-mxnet-py3-gpu**.

```
1 region = sagemaker_session.boto_session.region_name
2 mnist_estimator.train_image = lambda:'780728360657.dkr.ecr.{}.amazonaws.com/container-
      image:1.0'.format(region)
```

2. Insert the code before the call to `sagemaker.mxnet.MXNet.fit`, which sends a `CreateTrainingJob` request to Amazon SageMaker using the MXNet v0.11 container image. This overrides the default v0.12 image with the v0.11 image.

   The following shows a sample MXNet training code snippet with the new code highlighted.

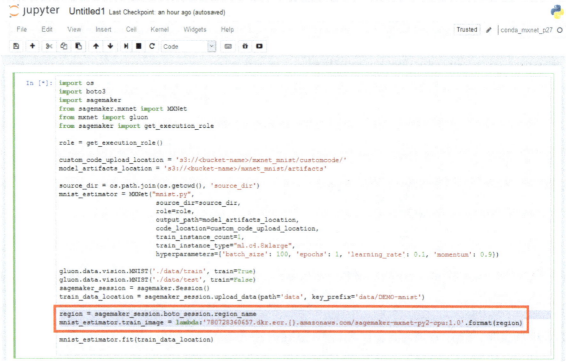

Now you can continue training the model as described in the Amazon SageMaker documentation.

How to Configure Machine Learning Inference Using the AWS Management Console

This feature is available for AWS Greengrass Core v1.5.0 only.

You can perform machine learning (ML) inference locally on a Greengrass core device using data from connected devices. For information, including requirements and constraints, see Perform Machine Learning Inference.

This tutorial describes how to use the AWS Management Console to configure a Greengrass group to run a Lambda inference app that recognizes images from a camera locally, without sending data to the cloud. The inference app accesses the camera module on a Raspberry Pi and runs inference using the open source SqueezeNet model.

The tutorial contains the following high-level steps:

1. Configure the Raspberry Pi

2. Install the MXNet Framework

3. Create a Model Package

4. Create and Publish a Lambda Function

5. Add the Lambda Function to the Group

6. Add Resources to the Group

7. Add a Subscription to the Group

8. Deploy the Group

Prerequisites

To complete this tutorial, you need:

- Raspberry Pi 3 Model B.
- Raspberry Pi Camera Module V2 - 8 Megapixel, 1080p. To learn how to set up the camera, see Connecting the camera in the Raspberry Pi documentation.
- A Greengrass group and a Greengrass core. To learn how to create a Greengrass group or core, see Getting Started with AWS Greengrass. The Getting Started section also includes steps for installing the AWS Greengrass Core software on a Raspberry Pi.

Note
This tutorial uses a Raspberry Pi, but AWS Greengrass supports other platforms, such as Intel Atom and NVIDIA Jetson TX2.

Step 1: Configure the Raspberry Pi

In this step, you update the Rasbian operating system, install the camera module software and Python dependencies, and enable the camera interface. Run the following commands in your Raspberry Pi terminal.

1. Update Raspbian Jessie.

```
1 sudo apt-get update
2 sudo apt-get dist-upgrade
```

2. Install the picamera interface for the camera module and other Python libraries that are required for this tutorial.

```
1 sudo apt-get install -y python-dev python-setuptools python-pip python-picamera
```

3. Reboot the Raspberry Pi.

```
1 sudo reboot
```

4. Open the Raspberry Pi configuration tool.

```
1 sudo raspi-config
```

5. Use the arrow keys to open **Interfacing Options** and enable the camera interface. If prompted, allow the device to reboot.

6. Use the following command to test the camera setup.

```
1 raspistill -v -o test.jpg
```

This opens a preview window on the Raspberry Pi, saves a picture named `test.jpg` to your /home/pi directory, and displays information about the camera in the Raspberry Pi terminal.

Step 2: Install the MXNet Framework

In this step, you download precompiled Apache MXNet libraries and install them on your Raspberry Pi.

Note
This tutorial uses libraries for the MXNet ML framework, but libraries for TensorFlow are also available. For more information, including limitations, see Precompiled Libraries for ML Frameworks.

1. On your computer, open the AWS IoT console.

2. In the left pane, choose **Software**.

3. In the **Machine learning libraries** section, for ** MXNet/TensorFlow precompiled libraries**, choose **Configure download**.

4. On the **Machine learning libraries** page, under **Software configurations**, for MXNet Raspberry Pi version 0.11.0, choose **Download**. **Note**
   By downloading this software you agree to the Apache License 2.0.

5. Transfer the downloaded `ggc-mxnet-v0.11.0-python-raspi.tar.gz` file from your computer to your Raspberry Pi. **Note**
   For ways that you can do this on different platforms, see this step in the Getting Started section. For example, you might use the following `scp` command:

```
1  scp ggc-mxnet-v0.11.0-python-raspi.tar.gz pi@IP-address:/home/pi
```

6. In your Raspberry Pi terminal, unpack the transferred file.

```
1  tar -xzf ggc-mxnet-v0.11.0-python-raspi.tar.gz
```

7. Install the MDXNet framework.

```
1  ./mxnet_installer.sh
```

Note
You can continue to Step 3: Create an MXNet Model Package while the framework is installing, but you must wait for the installation to complete before proceeding to Step 4: Create and Publish a Lambda Function.
You can optionally run unit tests to verify the installation. To do so, add the `-u` option to the previous command. If successful, each test logs a line in the terminal that ends with `ok`. If all tests are successful, the final log statement contains `OK`. Note that running the unit tests increases the installation time.

The script also creates a Lambda function deployment package named `greengrassObjectClassification.zip`. This package contains the function code and dependencies, including the **mxnet** Python module that Greengrass Lambda functions need to work with MXNet models. You upload this deployment package later.

1. When the installation is complete, transfer `greengrassObjectClassification.zip` to your computer. Depending on your environment, you can use the `scp` command or a utility such as WinSCP.

Step 3: Create an MXNet Model Package

In this step, you download files for a sample pretrained MXNet model, and then save them as a `.zip` file. AWS Greengrass can use models from Amazon S3, provided that they use the `tar.gz` or `.zip` format.

1. Download the following files to your computer:
   - squeezenet_v1.1-0000.params. A parameter file that describes weights of the connectivity.
   - squeezenet_v1.1-symbol.json. A symbol file that describes the neural network structure.
   - synset.txt. A synset file that maps recognized class IDs to human-readable class names. **Note**
     All MXNet model packages use these three file types, but the contents of TensorFlow model packages vary.

2. Zip the three files, and name the compressed file **squeezenet.zip**. You upload this model package to Amazon S3 in Step 6: Add Resources to the Greengrass Group.

Step 4: Create and Publish a Lambda Function

In this step, you create a Lambda function and configure it to use the deployment package that was created in Step 2: Install the MXNet Framework. Then, you publish a function version and create an alias.

The Lambda function deployment package is named `greengrassObjectClassification.zip`. It contains an inference app that performs common tasks, such as loading models, importing Apache MXNet, and taking actions based on predictions. The app contains the following key components:

- App logic:
    - **load_model.py**. Loads MXNet models.
    - **greengrassObjectClassification.py**. Runs predictions on images that are streamed from the camera.
- Dependencies:
    - **greengrasssdk**. Required library for all Python Lambda functions.
    - **mxnet**. Required library for Python Lambda functions that run local inference using MXNet.
- License:
    - **license**. Contains the required Greengrass Core Software License Agreement.

Note
You can reuse these dependencies and license when you create new MXNet inference Lambda functions.

First, create the Lambda function.

1. In the AWS IoT console, in the left pane, choose **Greengrass**, and then choose **Groups**.

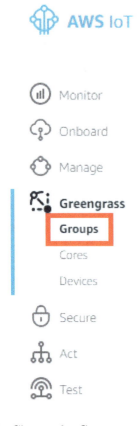

2. Choose the Greengrass group where you want to add the Lambda function.

3. On the group configuration page, choose **Lambdas**, and then choose **Add Lambda**.

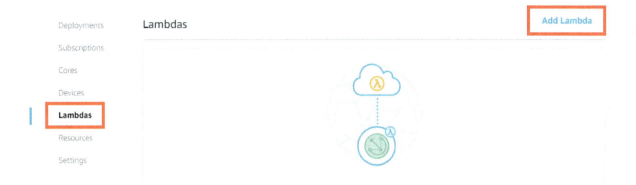

4. On the **Add a Lambda to your Greengrass Group** page, choose **Create new Lambda**. This takes you to the AWS Lambda console.

5. Choose **Author from scratch**.

6. In the **Author from scratch** section, use the following values:
   [See the AWS documentation website for more details]

7. At the bottom of the page, choose **Create function**.

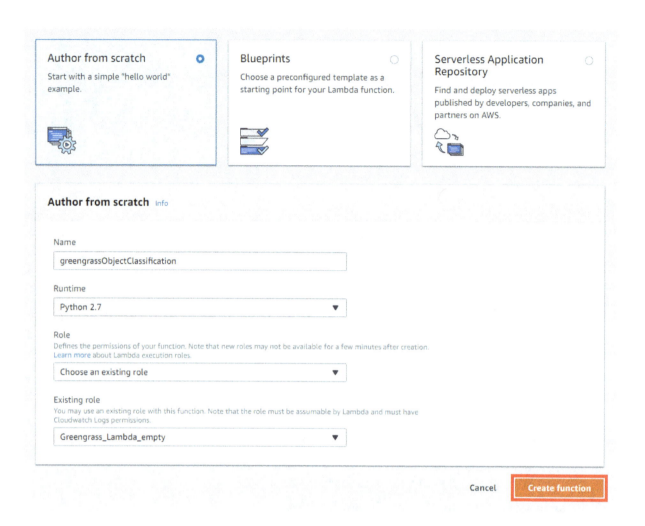

Now, upload your Lambda function deployment package and register the handler.

1. On the **Configuration** tab for the **greengrassObjectClassification** function, use the following values for **Function code**:
   [See the AWS documentation website for more details]

2. Choose **Upload**.

3. Choose your `greengrassObjectClassification.zip` deployment package.

4. At the top of the page, choose **Save**.

Next, publish the first version of your Lambda function. Then, create an alias for the version.

Note

Greengrass groups can reference a Lambda function by alias (recommended) or by version. Using an alias makes it easier to manage code updates because you don't have to change your subscription table or group definition when the function code is updated. Instead, you just point the alias to the new function version.

1. From the **Actions** menu, choose **Publish new version**.

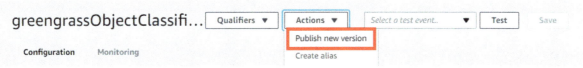

2. For **Version description**, type **First version**, and then choose **Publish**.

3. On the **greengrassObjectClassification: 1** configuration page, from the **Actions** menu, choose **Create alias**.

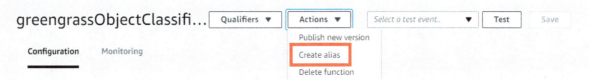

4. On the **Create a new alias** page, use the following values:
   [See the AWS documentation website for more details] **Note**
   AWS Greengrass doesn't support Lambda aliases for **$LATEST** versions.

5. Choose **Create**.

An alias is a pointer to one or two versions. Select the version(s) you would like the alias to point to.

Name*

    mlTest

Description

Version*

    1   ▼

You can shift traffic between two versions, based on weights (%) that you assign. Click here to learn more.

Additional Version

                                           ▼

                                      Cancel   **Create**

Now, add the Lambda function to your Greengrass group.

Step 5: Add the Lambda Function to the Greengrass Group

In this step, you add the Lambda function to the group and then configure its lifecycle.

First, add the Lambda function to your Greengrass group.

1. In the AWS IoT console, open the group configuration page.

2. Choose **Lambdas**, and then choose **Add Lambda**.

3. On the **Add a Lambda to your Greengrass Group** page, choose **Use existing Lambda**.

4. On the **Use existing Lambda** page, choose **greengrassObjectClassification**, and then choose **Next**.

5. On the **Select a Lambda version** page, choose **Alias:mlTest**, and then choose **Finish**.

Next, configure the lifecycle of the Lambda function.

1. On the **Lambdas** page, choose the **greengrassObjectClassification** Lambda function.

2. On the **greengrassObjectClassification** configuration page, choose **Edit**.

3. On the **Group-specific Lambda configuration** page, use the following values:
[See the AWS documentation website for more details] **Note**
A *long-lived*—or *pinned*—Lambda function starts automatically after AWS Greengrass starts and keeps running in its own container (or sandbox). This is in contrast to an *on-demand* Lambda function, which starts only when invoked and stops when there are no tasks left to execute. When possible, you should use on-demand Lambda functions because they are less resource intensive than long-lived functions. However, the Lambda function in this tutorial requires a long-lived lifecycle.

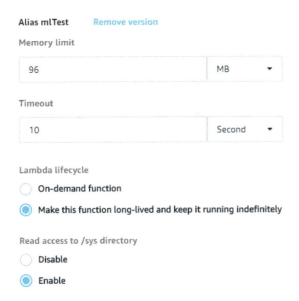

Alias mlTest   Remove version

Memory limit

| 96 | MB ▾ |

Timeout

| 10 | Second ▾ |

Lambda lifecycle

○ On-demand function

◉ Make this function long-lived and keep it running indefinitely

Read access to /sys directory

○ Disable

◉ Enable

4. At the bottom of the page, choose **Update**.

Step 6: Add Resources to the Greengrass Group

In this step, you create resources for the camera module and the ML inference model. You also affiliate the resources with the Lambda function, which enables the function to access the resources on the core device.

First, create two local device resources for the camera: one for shared memory and one for the device interface. For more information about local resource access, see Access Local Resources with Lambda Functions.

1. On the group configuration page, choose **Resources**.

Deployments

Subscriptions

Cores

Devices

Lambdas

Resources

Settings

2. For **Local resources**, choose **Add**.

3. On the **Create a local resource** page, use the following values:
   [See the AWS documentation website for more details]

The **Device path** is the local absolute path of the device resource. This path can only refer to a character device or block device under /dev.

The **Group owner file access permission** option lets you grant additional file access permissions to the Lambda process. For more information, see Group Owner File Access Permission.

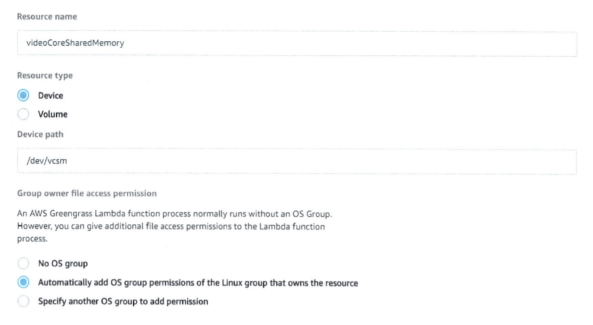

4. Under **Lambda function affiliations**, choose **Select**.

5. Choose **greengrassObjectClassification**, choose **Read and write access**, and then choose **Done**.

Next, you add a local device resource for the camera interface.

6. At the bottom of the page, choose **Add another resource**.

7. On the **Create a local resource** page, use the following values:
[See the AWS documentation website for more details]

8. Under **Lambda function affiliations**, choose **Select**.

9. Choose **greengrassObjectClassification**, choose **Read and write access**, and then choose **Done**.

10. At the bottom of the page, choose **Save**.

Now, add the inference model as a machine learning resource. This step includes uploading the `squeezenet.zip` model package to Amazon S3.

1. For **Machine learning resources**, choose **Add**.

2. On the **Create a machine learning resource** page, for **Resource name**, type **squeezenet_model**.

3. For **Model source**, choose **Locate or upload a model in S3**.

4. Under **Model from S3**, choose **Select**, and then choose **Create S3 bucket**.

5. For **Bucket name**, type a name that contains the string **greengrass** (such as **greengrass-*datetime***), and then choose **Create. Note**
Don't use a period (".") in the bucket name.

6. Choose **Upload a model**, and then choose the `squeezenet.zip` package that you created in Step 3: Create an MXNet Model Package.

7. For **Local path**, type **/greengrass-machine-learning/mxnet/squeezenet**.

This is the destination for the local model in the Lambda runtime namespace. When you deploy the group, AWS Greengrass retrieves the source model package and then extracts the contents to the specified directory. The sample Lambda function for this tutorial is already configured to use this path (in the `model_path` variable).

8. Under **Lambda function affiliations**, choose **Select**.

9. Choose **greengrassObjectClassification**, choose **Read-only access**, and then choose **Done**.

10. At the bottom of the page, choose **Save**.

Using Amazon SageMaker Trained Models

This tutorial uses a model that's stored in Amazon S3, but you can easily use Amazon SageMaker models too. The Greengrass console has built-in Amazon SageMaker integration, so you don't need to manually upload these models to Amazon S3. For requirements and limitations for using Amazon SageMaker models, see Supported Model Sources.

To use an Amazon SageMaker model:

- For **Model source**, choose **Use an existing SageMaker model**, and then choose the name of the model's training job.
- For **Local path**, type the path to the directory where your Lambda function looks for the model.

Step 7: Add a Subscription to the Greengrass Group

In this step, you add a subscription to the group. This subscription enables the Lambda function to send prediction results to AWS IoT by publishing to an MQTT topic.

1. On the group configuration page, choose **Subscriptions**, and then choose **Add Subscription**.

2. On the **Select your source and target** page, configure the source and target, as follows:

   1. In **Select a source**, choose **Lambdas**, and then choose **greengrassObjectClassification**.

   2. In **Select a target**, choose **Services**, and then choose **IoT Cloud**.

   3. Choose **Next**.

3. On the **Filter your data with a topic** page, in the **Optional topic filter** field, type **hello/world**, and then choose **Next**.

4. Choose **Finish**.

Step 8: Deploy the Greengrass Group

In this step, you deploy the current version of the group definition to the Greengrass core device. The definition contains the Lambda function, resources, and subscription configurations that you added.

1. Make sure that the AWS Greengrass core is running. Run the following commands in your Raspberry Pi terminal, as needed.

    1. To check whether the daemon is running:

```
1 ps aux | grep -E 'greengrass.*daemon'
```

   If the output contains a **root** entry for **/greengrass/ggc/packages/1.5.0/bin/daemon**, then the daemon is running. **Note**
   The version in the path depends on the AWS Greengrass Core software version that's installed on your core device.

    2. To start the daemon:

```
1 cd /greengrass/ggc/core/
2 sudo ./greengrassd start
```

2. On the group configuration page, choose **Deployments**, and from the **Actions** menu, choose **Deploy**.

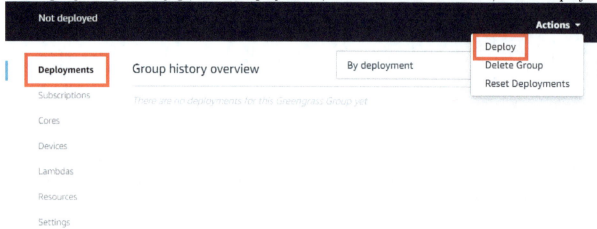

3. On the **Configure how devices discover your core** page, choose **Automatic detection**.

   This enables devices to automatically acquire connectivity information for the core, such as IP address, DNS, and port number. Automatic detection is recommended, but AWS Greengrass also supports manually specified endpoints. You're only prompted for the discovery method the first time that the group is deployed.

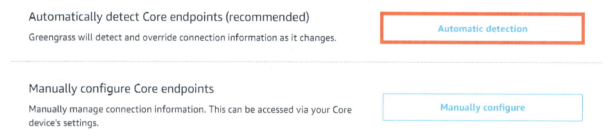

   Note

   If prompted, grant permission to create the AWS Greengrass service role on your behalf, which allows AWS Greengrass to access other AWS services. You need to do this only one time per account.

   The **Deployments** page shows the deployment time stamp, version ID, and status. When completed, the deployment should show a **Successfully completed** status.

Test the Inference App

Now you can verify whether the deployment is configured correctly. To test, you subscribe to the **hello/world** topic and view the prediction results that are published by the Lambda function.

Note
If a monitor is attached to the Raspberry Pi, the live camera feed is displayed in a preview window.

1. On the AWS IoT console home page, choose **Test**.

2. For **Subscriptions**, use the following values:
   [See the AWS documentation website for more details]

3. Choose **Subscribe to topic**.

   If the test is successful, the messages from the Lambda function appear at the bottom of the page. Each message contains the top five prediction results of the image, using the format: probability, predicted class ID, and corresponding class name.

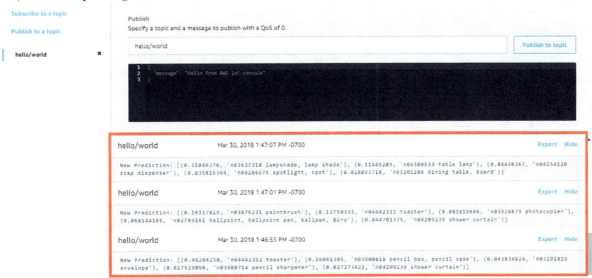

Troubleshooting AWS Greengrass ML Inference

If the test is not successful, you can try the following troubleshooting steps. Run the commands in your Raspberry Pi terminal.

Check Error Logs

1. Switch to the root user.

```
1 sudo su
```

2. Navigate to the /log directory.

```
1 cd /greengrass/ggc/var/log
```

3. Check `runtime.log` or `python_runtime.log`.

   For more information, see Troubleshooting with Logs.

"Unpacking" Error in runtime.log

If `runtime.log` contains an error similar to the following, ensure that your `tar.gz` source model package has a parent directory.

```
1 Greengrass deployment error: unable to download the artifact model-arn: Error while processing.
2 Error while unpacking the file from /tmp/greengrass/artifacts/model-arn/path to /greengrass/ggc/
      deployment/path/model-arn,
3 error: open /greengrass/ggc/deployment/path/model-arn/squeezenet/squeezenet_v1.1-0000.params: no
      such file or directory
```

If your package doesn't have a parent directory that contains the model files, try repackaging the model using the following command:

```
1 tar -zcvf model.tar.gz ./model
```

For example:

```
1
2 $ tar -zcvf test.tar.gz ./test
3 ./test
4 ./test/some.file
5 ./test/some.file2
6 ./test/some.file3
```

Note
Don't include trailing `/*` characters in this command.

Verify That the Lambda Function Is Successfully Deployed

1. List the contents of the deployed Lambda in the /lambda directory. Replace the placeholder values before running the command.

```
1 cd /greengrass/ggc/deployment/lambda/arn:aws:lambda:region:account:function:function-name:
      function-version
2 ls -la
```

2. Verify that the directory contains the same content as the **greengrassObjectClassification.zip** deployment package that you uploaded in Step 4: Create and Publish a Lambda Function.

   Also make sure that the `.py` files and dependencies are in the root of the directory.

Verify That the Inference Model Is Successfully Deployed

1. Find the process identification number (PID) of the Lambda runtime process:

```
1 ps aux | grep lambda-function-name
```

   In the output, the PID appears in the second column of the line for the Lambda runtime process.

2. Enter the Lambda runtime namespace. Be sure to replace the placeholder *pid* value before running the command. **Note**
   This directory and its contents are in the Lambda runtime namespace, so they aren't visible in a regular Linux namespace.

```
1 sudo nsenter -t pid -m /bin/bash
```

3. List the contents of the local directory that you specified for the ML resource.

```
1 cd /greengrass-machine-learning/mxnet/squeezenet/
2 ls -ls
```

   You should see the following files:

```
1 32 -rw-r--r-- 1 ggc_user ggc_group   31675 Nov 18 15:19 synset.txt
2 32 -rw-r--r-- 1 ggc_user ggc_group   28707 Nov 18 15:19 squeezenet_v1.1-symbol.json
3 4832 -rw-r--r-- 1 ggc_user ggc_group 4945062 Nov 18 15:19 squeezenet_v1.1-0000.params
```

Next Steps

Next, explore other inference apps. AWS Greengrass provides other Lambda functions that you can use to try out local inference. You can find the examples package in the precompiled libraries folder that you downloaded in Step 2: Install the MXNet Framework.

Configuring an NVIDIA Jetson TX2

To run this tutorial on the GPU of an NVIDIA Jetson TX2, you must add additional local device resources and configure access for the Lambda function.

Note
Your Jetson must be configured before you can install the AWS Greengrass Core software. For more information, see Configuring NVIDIA Jetson TX2 for AWS Greengrass.

1. Add the following local device resources. Follow the procedure in Add Resources to the Group.

   For each resource:

   - For **Resource type**, choose **Device**.
   - For **Group owner file access permission**, choose **Automatically add OS group permissions of the Linux group that owns the resource**.
   - For **Lambda function affiliations**, grant **Read and write access** to your Lambda function.

   [See the AWS documentation website for more details]

2. Edit the configuration of the Lambda function to increase **Memory limit** to 1000 MB. Follow the procedure in Add the Lambda Function to the Group.

Greengrass Discovery RESTful API

All devices that communicate with an AWS Greengrass core must be a member of a Greengrass group. Each group must have an AWS Greengrass core. The Discovery API enables devices to retrieve information required to connect to an AWS Greengrass core that is in the same Greengrass group as the device. When a device first comes online, it can connect to the AWS Greengrass cloud service and use the Discovery API to find:

- The group to which it belongs.
- The IP address and port for the AWS Greengrass core in the group.
- The group's root CA certificate, which can be used to authenticate the AWS Greengrass core device.

To use this API, send HTTP requests to the following URI:

```
1 https://your-aws-endpoint/greengrass/discover/thing/thing-name
```

The endpoint is specific to your AWS account. To retrieve your endpoint, use the `aws iot describe-endpoint` CLI command:

```
1 $ aws iot describe-endpoint
2 {
3     "endpointAddress": "a1b2c3d4e5f6g7.iot.us-west-2.amazonaws.com"
4 }
```

Use port 8443 when connecting. For a list of region-specific endpoints, see AWS IoT Regions and Endpoints in the *AWS General Reference*. This is a data plane only API. The endpoints used for working with rules, certificates, and policies do not support the Discovery API.

Request

The request contains the standard HTTP headers and is sent to the following URI:

```
1 HTTP GET https://your-aws-endpoint/greengrass/discover/thing/thingName
```

Response

Response

Upon success, the response includes the standard HTTP headers plus the following code and body:

```
1 HTTP 200
2 BODY: response document
```

For more information see, Example Discover Response Documents.

Authorization

Retrieving the connectivity information requires a policy that allows the caller to perform the `greengrass:Discover` action. TLS mutual authentication with a client certificate is the only accepted form of authentication. The following is an example policy that allows a caller to perform this action:

```
1 {
2     "Version": "2012-10-17",
3     "Statement": [{
4         "Effect": "Allow",
5         "Action": "greengrass:Discover",
```

```
6        "Resource": ["arn:aws:iot:aws-region:aws-account:thing/thing-name"]
7      }]
8  }
```

Example Discover Response Documents

The following document shows the response for a device that is a member of a group with one AWS Greengrass core, one endpoint, and one group CA:

```
1  {
2    "GGGroups": [
3      {
4        "GGGroupId": "gg-group-01-id",
5        "Cores": [
6          {
7            "thingArn": "core-01-thing-arn",
8            "Connectivity": [
9              {
10               "id": "core-01-connection-id",
11               "hostAddress": "core-01-address",
12               "portNumber": core-01-port,
13               "metadata": "core-01-description"
14             }
15           ]
16         }
17       ],
18       "CAs": [
19         "-----BEGIN CERTIFICATE-----cert-contents-----END CERTIFICATE-----"
20       ]
21     }
22   ]
23 }
```

The following document shows the response for a device that is a member of two groups with one AWS Greengrass core, multiple endpoints, and multiple group CAs:

```
1  {
2    "GGGroups": [
3      {
4        "GGGroupId": "gg-group-01-id",
5        "Cores": [
6          {
7            "thingArn": "core-01-thing-arn",
8            "Connectivity": [
9              {
10               "id": "core-01-connection-id",
11               "hostAddress": "core-01-address",
12               "portNumber": core-01-port,
13               "metadata": "core-01-connection-1-description"
14             },
15             {
16               "id": "core-01-connection-id-2",
17               "hostAddress": "core-01-address-2",
18               "portNumber": core-01-port-2,
```

```
19              "metadata": "core-01-connection-2-description"
20            }
21          ]
22        }
23      ],
24      "CAs": [
25        "-----BEGIN CERTIFICATE-----cert-contents-----END CERTIFICATE-----",
26        "-----BEGIN CERTIFICATE-----cert-contents-----END CERTIFICATE-----",
27        "-----BEGIN CERTIFICATE-----cert-contents-----END CERTIFICATE-----"
28      ]
29    },
30    {
31      "GGGroupId": "gg-group-02-id",
32      "Cores": [
33        {
34          "thingArn":"core-02-thing-arn",
35          "Connectivity" : [
36          {
37            "id": "core-02-connection-id",
38            "hostAddress": "core-02-address",
39            "portNumber": core-02-port,
40            "metadata": "core-02-connection-1-description"
41          }
42          ],
43          "CAs": [
44              "-----BEGIN CERTIFICATE-----cert-contents-----END CERTIFICATE-----",
45              "-----BEGIN CERTIFICATE-----cert-contents-----END CERTIFICATE-----",
46              "-----BEGIN CERTIFICATE-----cert-contents-----END CERTIFICATE-----"
47          ]
48        }
49      ]
50    }
51 }
```

Note

An AWS Greengrass group must define exactly one AWS Greengrass core. Any response from the AWS Greengrass cloud service that contains a list of AWS Greengrass cores only contains one AWS Greengrass core.

Use Greengrass OPC-UA to Communicate with Industrial Equipment

Greengrass supports OPC-UA, an information exchange standard for industrial communication. OPC-UA allows you to ingest and process messages from industrial equipment and deliver them to devices in your Greengrass group or to the cloud based on rules you define.

The Greengrass implementation of OPC-UA supports certificate-based authentication. It is based on an open source implementation, and is fully customizable. You can also bring your own implementation of OPC-UA, and implement your own support for other custom, legacy, and proprietary messaging protocols.

In this section we will cover the following steps:

- Connect to an existing OPC-UA server.
- Monitor an existing OPC-UA node within that server.
- Get called back when the monitored node's value changes.

Architectural Overview

Greengrass implements OPC-UA as a Lambda function in NodeJS. Since Lambda functions running on Greengrass cores have access to network resources, you can create Lambda functions that proxy information from your existing OPC-UA servers over TCP to other functions or services in your Greengrass group.

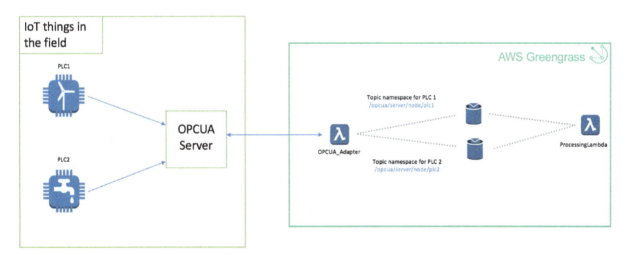

You can configure Greengrass to have a long-lived connection to your OPC-UA server(s), and, using OPC-UA Subscriptions, you can have your OPCUA_Adapter Lambda function monitor changes to pre-defined nodes. Any change to those nodes triggers a Publish event from the OPC-UA server, which will be received by your Lambda function, and republished into predefined topic names.

The topic structure is constructed as follows:

```
14 const configSet = {
15     server: {
16         name: 'server1',
17         url: 'opc.tcp://localhost:24567',
18     },
19     subscriptions: [
20         {
21             name: 'MyTemperature1',
22             nodeId: 'ns=1;s=Temperature',
23         },
24     ],
25 };
```

`/opcua/server1/node/MyTemperature1`

Set Up a Test OPC-UA Server

Use the following commands to set up a test OPC-UA server. Or, if you already have an OPC-UA server you'd like to use instead, you may skip this step.

```
1 git clone git://github.com/node-opcua/node-opcua.git
2 cd node-opcua
3 git checkout v0.0.64
4 npm install
5 node bin/simple_server
```

The server produces the following output:

```
1 [ec2-user@<your_instance_id> node-opcua]$ node bin/simple_server
2   server PID            : 28585
3
4 registering server to :opc.tcp://<your_instance_id>4840/UADiscovery
5 err Cannot find module 'usage'
6 skipping installation of cpu_usage and memory_usage nodes
7   server on port       : 26543
8   endpointUrl          : opc.tcp://<your_instance_id>us-west-2.compute.internal:26543
9   serverInfo           :
10      applicationUri               : urn:54f7890cca4c49a1:NodeOPCUA-Server
11      productUri                   : NodeOPCUA-Server
12      applicationName              : locale=en text=NodeOPCUA
13      applicationType              : SERVER
14      gatewayServerUri             : null
15      discoveryProfileUri          : null
16      discoveryUrls                :
17      productName                  : NODEOPCUA-SERVER
18  buildInfo        :
19      productUri                   : NodeOPCUA-Server
20      manufacturerName             : Node-OPCUA : MIT Licence ( see http://node-opcua.github.
           io/)
21      productName                  : NODEOPCUA-SERVER
22      softwareVersion              : 0.0.65
23      buildNumber                  : 1234
24      buildDate                    : Thu Aug 03 2017 00:13:50 GMT+0000 (UTC)
25
26  server now waiting for connections. CTRL+C to stop
```

Make sure your Greengrass Group is ready

- Create a Greengrass group (find more details in Configure AWS Greengrass on AWS IoT.)
- Set up a Greengrass Core on one of the supported platforms (Raspberry-pi for example)
- Set up your Greengrass Core to be able to run nodejs6.x Lambda functions

Use Greengrass OPC-UA to Interact with your OPC-UA Server

1. Prepare your Lambda function

   Get the code for an OPC-UA adapter Lambda function from GitHub:

```
1 git clone https://github.com/aws-samples/aws-greengrass-samples.git
2 cd aws-greengrass-samples/greengrass-opcua-adapter-nodejs
3 npm install
```

   Note: This Lambda function uses the node-opcua library (v0.0.64), which attempts to re-generate some model files at runtime. That doesn't work when running as a Lambda function on Greengrass, because Lambda functions start with a Read-Only file system, so any code trying to generate other code would not work. The next step fixes this.

2. Change the file at `node_modules/node-opcua/lib/misc/factories.js`: line 109 to this:

```
1 var generated_source_is_outdated = (!generated_source_exists);
```

   Run this command to make that change:

```
1 sed -i '109s/.*/    var generated_source_is_outdated = (!generated_source_exists);/'
      node_modules/node-opcua/lib/misc/factories.js
```

3. Configure the server and monitored nodes

   Change the `configSet` variable inside the `index.js` file of the OPC-UA Lambda function to contain the server IP and Port that you want to connect to, as well as the node Ids you would like to monitor. By default it comes with the following example configuration:

```
1  const configSet = {
2      server: {
3          name: 'server',
4          url: 'opc.tcp://localhost:26543',
5      },
6      subscriptions: [
7          {
8          name: 'MyPumpSpeed',
9          nodeId: 'ns=1;s=PumpSpeed',
10          },
11      ],
12 };
```

   In this case, we are connecting to an OPC-UA server running on the same host as our Greengrass Core, on port 26543, and monitoring one node that has an OPC-UA Id 'ns=1;s=PumpSpeed'.

4. Configure the authentication mode

   The OPC-UA library used in this example supports three modes of Authentication to your OPC-UA server. The most secure method is Certificate Based Authentication, but the library also allows you to specify username/password or no authentication.

   Here is how to set Certificate Based Authentication:

- Package your certificate and private key with your Lambda function, for example under a directory named `certs/`.

- Change the `clientOptions` variable to contain certificateFile, privateKeyFile and securityModes, securityPolicies options:

```
1 const clientOptions = {
2     keepSessionAlive: true,
3     certificateFile: /lambda/certs/<certificate_name>.pem.crt,
4     privateKeyFile: /lambda/certs/<private_key_name>.pem.key,
5     securityModes: MessageSecurityMode.SIGN,
6     securityPolicies: SecurityPolicy.BASIC256,
7     connectionStrategy: {
8         maxRetry: 1000000,
9         initialDelay: 2000,
10        maxDelay: 10 * 1000,
11    },
12 };
```

5. Upload your Lambda

   Create a Greengrass Lambda function. You can find more details on how to do that in Configure the Lambda Function for AWS Greengrass. In a nutshell, create a Lambda function code archive by doing the following:

```
1 # Download the nodejs greengrass sdk from
2 #   https://console.aws.amazon.com/iotv2/home?region=us-east-1#/software/greengrass/sdk.
3
4 #  Install Greengrass SDK in the node_modules directory
5 tar -zxvf aws-greengrass-core-sdk-js-*.tar.gz -C /tmp/
6 unzip /tmp/aws_greengrass_core_sdk_js/sdk/aws-greengrass-core-sdk.zip -d node_modules
7
8 # Archive the whole directory as a zip file
9 zip -r opcuaLambda.zip * -x \*.git\*
10
11 # Create an AWS Lambda with the created zip
12 aws lambda create-function --function-name <Function_Name> --runtime 'nodejs6.10' --role <
      Your_Role> --handler 'index.handler' --zip-file opcuaLambda.zip
```

   Add this Lambda to your Greengrass Group. Details are, again, in: Configure the Lambda Function for AWS Greengrass.

6. Configure and Deploy the Lambda function to your Greengrass Group

   After creating your AWS Lambda function, you add it to your Greengrass Group. Follow the instructions in same section as above.

   - Make sure to specify the Lambda function as Long-Running.
   - Give it at least 64MB of memory size.

   You can now create a deployment with your latest configuration. You can find details in Deploy Cloud Configurations to an AWS Greengrass Core Device.

Verify that your Lambda function is receiving OPC-UA Publishes and posting them onto Greengrass

As described in the Architecture section, your Lambda function should start receiving messages from your OPC-UA server. If you are using your own custom OPC-UA server, make sure you trigger a change in the

OPC-UA node Id you specified, so that you see the change received by your Lambda function. If you are using the example server above, the PumpSpeed node is configured to simulate a series of consecutive updates, so you should expect your Lambda function to receive multiple messages a second.

You can see messages received by your Lambda function in one of two ways:

- Watch the Lambda function's logs

  You can view the logs from your Lambda function by running the following command:

  ```
  1  sudo cat ggc/var/log/user/us-west-2/your_account_id/your_function_name.log
  ```

  The logs should look similar to:

  ```
  1  [2017-11-14T16:33:09.05Z][INFO]-started subscription : 305964
  2
  3  [2017-11-14T16:33:09.05Z][INFO]-monitoring node id =  ns=1;s=PumpSpeed
  4
  5  [2017-11-14T16:33:09.099Z][INFO]-monitoredItem initialized
  6
  7  [2017-11-15T23:49:34.752Z][INFO]-Publishing message on topic "/opcua/server/node/
        MyPumpSpeed" with Payload "{"id":"ns=1;s=PumpSpeed","value":{"dataType":"Double","
        arrayType":"Scalar","value":237.5250759433095}}"
  ```

- Configure Greengrass to forward messages from your Lambda function to the IoT Cloud.

  Follow the steps outlined in Verify the Lambda Function Is Running on the Device to receive messages on the AWS IoT console.

Note:

- Make sure there is a Subscription from your Lambda function going to the IoT Cloud. Details are in Configure the Lambda Function for AWS Greengrass.
- Since messages are forwarded to the cloud, make sure you terminate either the example server you configured above, or stop the Greengrass core, so that you don't end up publishing a lot of messages to IoT cloud and getting charged for them!

Next Steps

With Greengrass, you can use this same architecture to create your own implementation of OPC-UA, and also implement your own support for custom, legacy, and proprietary messaging protocols. Since Lambda functions running on Greengrass cores have access to network resources, you can use them to implement support for any protocol that rides on top of TCP-IP. In addition, you can also take advantage of Greengrass Local Resource Access to implement support for protocols that need access to hardware adapters/drivers.

AWS Greengrass Security

AWS Greengrass uses X.509 certificates, managed subscriptions, AWS IoT policies, and IAM policies and roles to ensure your Greengrass applications are secure. AWS Greengrass core devices require an AWS IoT thing, a device certificate, and an AWS IoT policy to communicate with the Greengrass cloud service.

This allows AWS Greengrass core devices to securely connect to the AWS IoT cloud services. It also allows the Greengrass cloud service to deploy configuration information, Lambda functions, and managed subscriptions to AWS Greengrass core devices.

AWS IoT devices require an AWS IoT thing, a device certificate, and an AWS IoT policy to connect to the Greengrass service. This allows AWS IoT devices to use the Greengrass Discovery Service to find and connect to an AWS Greengrass core device. AWS IoT devices use the same device certificate used to connect to AWS IoT device gateway and AWS Greengrass core devices. The following diagram shows the components of the AWS Greengrass security model:

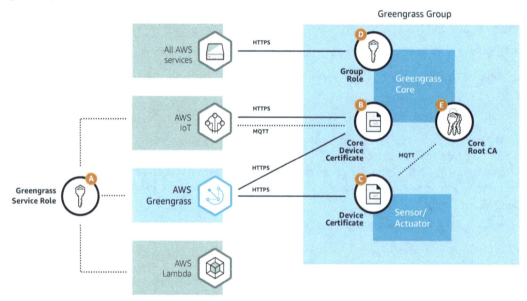

A - Greengrass service role
A customer-created IAM role that allows AWS Greengrass access to your AWS IoT and Lambda resources.

B - Core device certificate
An X.509 certificate used to authenticate an AWS Greengrass core.

C - Device certificate
An X.509 certificate used to authenticate an AWS IoT device.

D - Group role
A role assumed by AWS Greengrass when calling into the cloud from a Lambda function on an AWS Greengrass core.

E - Group CA
A root CA certificate used by AWS Greengrass devices to validate the certificate presented by an AWS Greengrass core device during TLS mutual authentication.

Configuring Greengrass Security

To configure your Greengrass application's security:

1. Create an AWS IoT thing for your AWS Greengrass core device.

2. Generate a key pair and device certificate for your AWS Greengrass core device.

3. Create and attach an AWS IoT policy to the device certificate. The certificate and policy allow the AWS Greengrass core device access to AWS IoT and Greengrass cloud services.

4. Create a Greengrass service role. This IAM role grants AWS Greengrass access to your Greengrass and AWS IoT resources. You only need to create a service role once per AWS account.

5. (Optional) Create a Greengrass group role. This role grants permission to Lambda functions running on an AWS Greengrass core to call other AWS services (in the cloud). You need to do this for each Greengrass group you create.

6. Create an AWS IoT thing for each device that will connect to your AWS Greengrass core.

7. Create device certificates, key pairs, and AWS IoT policies for each device that will connect to your AWS Greengrass core.

Note
You can also use existing AWS IoT things and certificates.

Device Connection Workflow

This section describes how devices connect to the AWS Greengrass cloud service and AWS Greengrass core devices.

- An AWS Greengrass core device uses its device certificate, private key, and the AWS IoT root CA certificate to connect to the Greengrass cloud service .
- The AWS Greengrass core device downloads group membership information from the Greengrass service.
- When a deployment is made to the AWS Greengrass core device, the Device Certificate Manager (DCM) handles certificate management for the AWS Greengrass core device.
- An AWS IoT device connects to the Greengrass cloud service using its device certificate, private key, and the AWS IoT root CA. After making the connection, the AWS IoT device uses the Greengrass Discovery Service to find the IP address of its AWS Greengrass core device. The device can also download the group's root CA certificate, which can be used to authenticate the Greengrass core device.
- An AWS IoT device attempts to connect to the AWS Greengrass core, passing its device certificate and client ID. If the client ID matches the thing name of the device and the certificate is valid, the connection is made. Otherwise, the connection is terminated.

Greengrass Messaging Workflow

A subscription table is used to define how messages are exchanged within a Greengrass group (between AWS Greengrass core devices, AWS IoT devices, and Lambda functions). Each entry in the subscription table specifies a source, a destination, and an MQTT topic over which messages are sent/received. Messages can be exchanged only if an entry exists in the subscription table specifying the source (message sender), the target (message recipient), and the MQTT topic. Subscription table entries specify passing messages in one direction, from the source to the target. If you want two-way message passing, create two subscription table entries, one for each direction.

MQTT Core Server Certificate Rotation

The MQTT core server certificate expires, by default, in 7 days. You can set the expiration to any value between 7 and 30 days. When the MQTT core server certificate expires, any attempt to validate the certificate fails. The device must be able to detect the failure and terminate the connection. Existing connections are not affected. When the certificate expires, the AWS Greengrass core device attempts to connect to the Greengrass cloud service to obtain a new certificate. If the connection is successful, the AWS Greengrass core device downloads a new MQTT core server certificate and restarts the local MQTT service. At this point, all AWS IoT devices connected to the core are disconnected.

If there is no internet connection when the AWS Greengrass core attempts to get a new MQTT core server certificate, AWS IoT devices are unable to connect to the AWS Greengrass core until the connection to the Greengrass cloud service is restored and a new MQTT core server certificate can be downloaded.

When AWS IoT devices are disconnected from a core, they have to wait a short period of time and then attempt to reconnect to the AWS Greengrass core device.

AWS Greengrass Cipher Suites

As opposed to the AWS IoT cloud, the AWS Greengrass core supports the following *local network* TLS cipher suites:

[See the AWS documentation website for more details]

Monitoring with AWS Greengrass Logs

AWS Greengrass consists of the cloud service and the AWS Greengrass core software. The core software can write logs to CloudWatch and to the local file system of your core device. Logging is configured at the group level.

All AWS Greengrass log entries include a time stamp, log level, and information about the event.

CloudWatch Logs

If you configure CloudWatch logging, you can view the logs on the **Logs** page of the Amazon CloudWatch console. Log groups for AWS Greengrass logs use the following naming conventions:

```
1 /aws/greengrass/GreengrassSystem/greengrass-system-component-name
2 /aws/greengrass/Lambda/aws-region/account-id/lambda-function-name
```

Under each log group, you see log streams with the following structure:

```
1 date/account-id/greengrass-group-id/name-of-core-that-generated-log
```

Be aware of the following considerations when using CloudWatch Logs:

- To enable logging to CloudWatch Logs, the following actions must be allowed in the AWS Greengrass group role:
  - logs:PutLogEvents
  - logs:CreateLogGroup
  - logs:CreateLogStream
  - logs:DescribeLogStreams
- Logs are sent to CloudWatch Logs with a limited number of retries in case there's no internet connectivity. After the retries are exhausted, the event is dropped.
- Transaction, memory, and other limitations apply. For more information, see Logging Limitations.

File System Logs

If you configure file system logging, the log files are stored under *greengrass-root*/ggc/var/log on the core device, with the following high-level directory structure:

```
1 greengrass-root/ggc/var/log
2     - crash.log
3     - system
4       - log files for each Greengrass system component
5     - user
6       - log files generated by each user-defined Lambda function
```

Note
By default, *greengrass-root* is the **/greengrass** directory.

Be aware of the following considerations when using file system logs:

- Reading AWS Greengrass logs on the file system requires root privileges.
- AWS Greengrass supports size-based rotation and automatic cleanup when the amount of log data is close to the configured limit.
- The **crash.log** file is available in file system logs only. This log isn't written to CloudWatch Logs.
- Disk usage limitations apply. For more information, see Logging Limitations.

Note
Logs for AWS Greengrass Core Software v1.0.0 are stored under the *greengrass-root*/var/log directory.

Default Logging Configuration

If logging settings aren't explicitly configured, AWS Greengrass uses the following default logging configuration after the first group deployment.

AWS Greengrass System Components

- Type - `FileSystem`
- Component - `GreengrassSystem`
- Level - `INFO`
- Space - `128 KB`

User-defined Lambda Functions

- Type - `FileSystem`
- Component - `Lambda`
- Level - `INFO`
- Space - `128 KB`

Note
Before the first deployment, only system components write logs to the file system because no user-defined Lambda functions are deployed.

Configure Logging for AWS Greengrass

You can use the AWS IoT console or the AWS Greengrass APIs to configure AWS Greengrass logging.

Note
To allow AWS Greengrass to write logs to CloudWatch Logs, your group role must allow the required CloudWatch Logs actions.

Configure Logging (Console)

You configure logging on the group's **Settings** page.

1. In the AWS IoT console, choose **Greengrass**, and then choose **Groups**.

2. Choose the group where you want to configure logging.

3. On the group configuration page, choose **Settings**.

4. Choose the logging location, as follows:

    - To configure CloudWatch logging, for **CloudWatch logs configuration**, choose **Edit**.
    - To configure file system logging, for **Local logs configuration**, choose **Edit**.

    You can configure logging for one location or both locations.

5. On the **Configure Group logging** page, choose **Add another log type**.

6. Choose the event source, as follows:

    - To log events from user-defined Lambda functions, choose **User Lambdas**.
    - To log events from AWS Greengrass system components, choose **Greengrass system**.

    You can choose one component or both components.

7. Choose **Update**.

8. Choose the lowest level of events that you want to log. Events below this threshold are filtered out and aren't stored.

9. For file system logs, specify a disk space limit.

10. Choose **Save**.

Configure Logging (API)

You can use AWS Greengrass logger APIs to configure logging programmatically. For example, use the http://docs.aws.amazon.com/greengrass/latest/apireference/createloggerdefinition-post.html action to create a logger definition based on a http://docs.aws.amazon.com/greengrass/latest/apireference/definitions-loggerdefinitionversion.html payload, which uses the following syntax:

```
1  {
2    "Loggers": [
3      {
4        "Id": "string",
5        "Type": "FileSystem|AWSCloudWatch",
6        "Component": "GreengrassSystem|Lambda",
7        "Level": "DEBUG|INFO|WARN|ERROR|FATAL",
8        "Space": "integer"
9      },
10     {
11       "Id": "string",
12       ...
13     }
14   ]
15 }
```

LoggerDefinitionVersion is an array of one or more http://docs.aws.amazon.com/greengrass/latest/apireference/definitions-logger.html objects that have the following properties:

Id
An identifier for the logger.

Type
The storage mechanism for log events. When `AWSCloudWatch` is used, log events are sent to CloudWatch Logs. When `FileSystem` is used, log events are stored on the local file system.
Valid values: `AWSCloudWatch`, `FileSystem`

Component
The source of the log event. When `GreengrassSystem` is used, events from Greengrass system components are logged. When `Lambda` is used, events from user-defined Lambda functions are logged.
Valid values: `GreengrassSystem`, `Lambda`

Level
The log-level threshold. Log events below this threshold are filtered out and aren't stored.
Valid values: `DEBUG`, `INFO` (recommended), `WARN`, `ERROR`, `FATAL`

Space
The maximum amount of local storage, in KB, to use for storing logs. This field applies only when `Type` is set to `FileSystem`.

Configuration Example

The following `LoggerDefinitionVersion` example specifies a logging configuration that:

- Turns on file system `ERROR` (and above) logging for AWS Greengrass system components.
- Turns on file system `INFO` (and above) logging for user-defined Lambda functions.

- Turns on CloudWatch `INFO` (and above) logging for user-defined Lambda functions.

```
 1 {
 2    "Name": "LoggingExample",
 3    "InitialVersion": {
 4      "Loggers": [
 5        {
 6          "Id": "1",
 7          "Component": "GreengrassSystem",
 8          "Level": "ERROR",
 9          "Space": 10240,
10          "Type": "FileSystem"
11        },
12        {
13          "Id": "2",
14          "Component": "Lambda",
15          "Level": "INFO",
16          "Space": 10240,
17          "Type": "FileSystem"
18        },
19        {
20          "Id": "3",
21          "Component": "Lambda",
22          "Level": "INFO",
23          "Type": "AWSCloudWatch"
24        }
25      ]
26    }
27 }
```

After you create a logger definition version, you can use its version ARN to create a group version before deploying the group.

Logging Limitations

AWS Greengrass has the following logging limitations.

Transactions per Second

When logging to CloudWatch is enabled, the logging component batches log events locally before sending them to CloudWatch, so you can log at a rate higher than five requests per second per log stream.

Memory

If AWS Greengrass is configured to send logs to CloudWatch and a Lambda function logs more than 5 MB/second for a prolonged period of time, the internal processing pipeline eventually fills up. The theoretical worst case is 6 MB per Lambda function.

Clock Skew

When logging to CloudWatch is enabled, the logging component signs requests to CloudWatch using the normal Signature Version 4 signing process. If the system time on the AWS Greengrass core device is out of sync by more than 15 minutes, then the requests are rejected.

Disk Usage

Use the following formula to calculate the total maximum amount of disk usage for logging.

```
1 greengrass-system-component-space * 8    // 7 if automatic IP detection is disabled
2   + 128KB                                // the internal log for the local logging component
3   + lambda-space * lambda-count          // different versions of a Lambda function are treated
        as one
```

Where:

`greengrass-system-component-space`
The maximum amount of local storage for the AWS Greengrass system component logs.

`lambda-space`
The maximum amount of local storage for Lambda logs.

`lambda-count`
The number of deployed Lambda functions.

Log Loss

If your AWS Greengrass core device is configured to log only to CloudWatch and there's no internet connectivity, you have no way to retrieve the logs currently in the memory.

When Lambda functions are terminated (for example, during deployment), a few seconds' worth of logs are not written to CloudWatch.

Troubleshooting AWS Greengrass Applications

Use the following information to help troubleshoot issues in AWS Greengrass.

Issues

Symptom	Solution
You see 403 Forbidden error on deployment in the logs.	Make sure the policy of the AWS Greengrass core in the cloud includes "greengrass:*" as an allowed action.
Device's shadow does not sync with the cloud.	Check that the AWS Greengrass core has permissions for "iot:UpdateThingShadow" and "iot:GetThingShadow" actions. Also see Troubleshooting Shadow Synchronization Timeout Issues.
The AWS Greengrass core software does not run on Raspberry Pi because user namespace is not enabled.	Run `rpi-update` to update. Raspbian has released a new kernel 4.9 that has user namespace enabled.
A `ConcurrentDeployment` error occurs when you run `create-deployment` for the first time.	A deployment might be in progress. You can run `get-deployment-history` to see if a deployment was created. If not, try creating the deployment again.
The AWS Greengrass core software does not start successfully.	[See the AWS documentation website for more details]
The greengrassd script displays: `unable to accept TCP connection. accept tcp [::]:8000: accept4: too many open files`.	The file descriptor limit for the AWS Greengrass core software has reached the threshold and must be increased. Use the following command: ulimit -n 2048 and restart the AWS Greengrass core software. In this example, the limit is increased to 2048. Choose a value appropriate for your use case.
You receive the following error: `Runtime execution error: unable to start lambda container. container_linux.go:259: starting container process caused "process_linux.go:345: container init caused \"rootfs_linux .go:50: preparing rootfs caused \\\" permission denied\\\"\""`	Either install AWS Greengrass directly under the root directory, or ensure that the /greengrass directory and its parent directories have execute permissions for everyone.
The deployment fails with the following error message: Greengrass is not authorized to assume the Service Role associated with this account.	Using the AWS CLI, check that an appropriate service role is associated with your account using AssociateServiceRoleToAccount and that the account has at least the AWSGreengrassResourceAccessRolePolicy permission applied.
The deployment doesn't finish.	Make sure that the AWS Greengrass daemon is running on your core device. Run the following commands in your core device terminal to check whether the daemon is running and start it, if needed. [See the AWS documentation website for more details]

Symptom	Solution
The deployment doesn't finish, and runtime.log contains multiple `wait 1s for container to stop` entries.	Restart the AWS Greengrass daemon by running the following commands in your core device terminal. cd /greengrass/ggc/core/sudo ./greengrassd stopsudo ./greengrassd start
You receive the following error: `Deployment guid of type NewDeployment for group guid failed error: Error while processing. group config is invalid: 112 or [119 0] don't have rw permission on the file: path`	Ensure that the owner group of the *path* directory has read and write permissions to the directory.

Troubleshooting with Logs

[GGC v1.5.0]

If logs are configured to be stored on the local file system, start looking in the following locations. Reading the logs on the file system requires root privileges.

`greengrass-root/ggc/var/log/crash.log`
Shows messages generated when an AWS Greengrass core crashes.

`greengrass-root/ggc/var/log/system/runtime.log`
Shows messages about which component failed.

`greengrass-root/ggc/var/log/system/`
Contains all logs from AWS Greengrass system components, such as the certificate manager and the connection manager. By using the messages in `ggc/var/log/system/` and `ggc/var/log/system/runtime.log`, you should be able to find out which error occurred in AWS Greengrass system components.

`greengrass-root/ggc/var/log/user/`
Contains all logs from user-defined Lambda functions. Check this folder to find error messages from your local Lambda functions.

Note
By default, *greengrass-root* is the `/greengrass` directory.

If the logs are configured to be stored on the cloud, use CloudWatch Logs to view log messages. Note that `crash.log` is found only in file system logs on the AWS Greengrass core device.

If AWS IoT is configured to write logs to CloudWatch, check those logs for information if connection errors occur when system components attempt to connect to AWS IoT.

For more information about AWS Greengrass logging, see Monitoring with AWS Greengrass Logs.

[GGC v1.3.0]

If logs are configured to be stored on the local file system, start looking in the following locations. Reading the logs on the file system requires root privileges.

`greengrass-root/ggc/var/log/crash.log`
Shows messages generated when an AWS Greengrass core crashes.

`greengrass-root/ggc/var/log/system/runtime.log`
Shows messages about which component failed.

`greengrass-root/ggc/var/log/system/`
Contains all logs from AWS Greengrass system components, such as the certificate manager and the connection manager. By using the messages in `ggc/var/log/system/` and `ggc/var/log/system/runtime.log`, you should be able to find out which error occurred in AWS Greengrass system components.

`greengrass-root/ggc/var/log/user/`
Contains all logs from user-defined Lambda functions. Check this folder to find error messages from your local Lambda functions.

Note
By default, *greengrass-root* is the `/greengrass` directory.

If the logs are configured to be stored on the cloud, use CloudWatch Logs to view log messages. Note that `crash.log` is found only in file system logs on the AWS Greengrass core device.

If AWS IoT is configured to write logs to CloudWatch, check those logs for information if connection errors occur when system components attempt to connect to AWS IoT.

For more information about AWS Greengrass logging, see Monitoring with AWS Greengrass Logs.

[GGC v1.1.0]

If logs are configured to be stored on the local file system, start looking in the following locations. Reading the logs on the file system requires root privileges.

`greengrass-root/ggc/var/log/crash.log`
Shows messages generated when an AWS Greengrass core crashes.

`greengrass-root/ggc/var/log/system/runtime.log`
Shows messages about which component failed.

`greengrass-root/ggc/var/log/system/`
Contains all logs from AWS Greengrass system components, such as the certificate manager and the connection manager. By using the messages in `ggc/var/log/system/` and `ggc/var/log/system/runtime.log`, you should be able to find out which error occurred in AWS Greengrass system components.

`greengrass-root/ggc/var/log/user/`
Contains all logs from user-defined Lambda functions. Check this folder to find error messages from your local Lambda functions.

Note
By default, *greengrass-root* is the `/greengrass` directory.

If the logs are configured to be stored on the cloud, use CloudWatch Logs to view log messages. Note that `crash.log` is found only in file system logs on the AWS Greengrass core device.

If AWS IoT is configured to write logs to CloudWatch, check those logs for information if connection errors occur when system components attempt to connect to AWS IoT.

For more information about AWS Greengrass logging, see Monitoring with AWS Greengrass Logs.

[GGC v1.0.0]

If logs are configured to be stored on the local file system, start looking in the following locations. Reading the logs on the file system requires root privileges.

`greengrass-root/var/log/crash.log`
Shows messages generated when an AWS Greengrass core crashes.

`greengrass-root/var/log/system/runtime.log`
Shows messages about which component failed.

`greengrass-root/var/log/system/`
Contains all logs from AWS Greengrass system components, such as the certificate manager and the connection manager. Using the messages in `var/log/system/` and `var/log/system/runtime.log`, you should be able to find out which error occurred in AWS Greengrass system components.

`greengrass-root/var/log/user/`
Contains all logs from user-defined Lambda functions. Check this folder to find error messages from your local Lambda functions.

Note
By default, *greengrass-root* is the **/greengrass** directory.

If AWS Greengrass is configured to write logs to CloudWatch, you can view log messages in the CloudWatch console. Note that `crash.log` is found only in file system logs on the AWS Greengrass core device.

If AWS IoT is configured to write logs to CloudWatch, check those logs for information if connection errors occur when system components attempt to connect to AWS IoT.

Troubleshooting Storage Issues

When the local file storage is full, some components might start failing:

- Local shadow updates do not occur.
- New AWS Greengrass core MQTT server certificates cannot be downloaded locally.
- Deployments fail.

You should always be aware of the amount of free space available locally. This can be calculated based on the sizes of deployed Lambda functions, the logging configuration (see Troubleshooting with Logs), and the number of shadows stored locally.

Troubleshooting Messages

All messages sent within AWS Greengrass are sent with QoS 0. If an AWS Greengrass core is restarted, messages that have not been processed yet are lost. For this reason, restart the AWS Greengrass core when the service disruption is the lowest. The AWS Greengrass core is restarted by a deployment, too.

Troubleshooting Shadow Synchronization Timeout Issues

[GGC v1.5.0]

If there is a significant delay in communication between a Greengrass core device and the cloud, then shadow synchronization may fail due to a timeout. You may see something like this in your log files:

```
1  [2017-07-20T10:01:58.006Z][ERROR]-cloud_shadow_client.go:57,Cloud shadow client error: unable to
       get cloud shadow what_the_thing_is_named for synchronization. Get https://1234567890abcd.
       iot.us-west-2.amazonaws.com:8443/things/what_the_thing_is_named/shadow: net/http: request
       canceled (Client.Timeout exceeded while awaiting headers)
```

```
2  [2017-07-20T10:01:58.006Z][WARN]-sync_manager.go:263,Failed to get cloud copy: Get https
       ://1234567890abcd.iot.us-west-2.amazonaws.com:8443/things/what_the_thing_is_named/shadow:
       net/http: request canceled (Client.Timeout exceeded while awaiting headers)
3  [2017-07-20T10:01:58.006Z][ERROR]-sync_manager.go:375,Failed to execute sync operation {
       what_the_thing_is_named VersionDiscontinued []}"
```

A possible fix is to configure the amount of time your Greengrass core device waits for a host response. Open the greengrass-root/config/config.json file and add a system.shadowSyncTimeout field with a timeout value in seconds. For example:

```
1  {
2    "coreThing": {
3      "caPath": "root-ca.pem",
4      "certPath": "cloud.pem.crt",
5      "keyPath": "cloud.pem.key",
6      "thingArn": "arn:aws:iot:us-west-2:049039099382:thing/GGTestGroup42_Core",
7      "iotHost": "your-AWS-IoT-endpoint",
8      "ggHost": "greengrass.iot.us-west-2.amazonaws.com",
9      "keepAlive": 600
10   },
11   "runtime": {
12     "cgroup": {
13       "useSystemd": "yes"
14     }
15   },
16   "system": {
17     "shadowSyncTimeout": 10
18   }
19 }
```

If no shadowSyncTimeout value is specified in the config.json file, the default is 1 second.

[GGC v1.3.0]

If there is a significant delay in communication between a Greengrass core device and the cloud, then shadow synchronization may fail due to a timeout. You may see something like this in your log files:

```
1  [2017-07-20T10:01:58.006Z][ERROR]-cloud_shadow_client.go:57,Cloud shadow client error: unable to
       get cloud shadow what_the_thing_is_named for synchronization. Get https://1234567890abcd.
       iot.us-west-2.amazonaws.com:8443/things/what_the_thing_is_named/shadow: net/http: request
       canceled (Client.Timeout exceeded while awaiting headers)
2  [2017-07-20T10:01:58.006Z][WARN]-sync_manager.go:263,Failed to get cloud copy: Get https
       ://1234567890abcd.iot.us-west-2.amazonaws.com:8443/things/what_the_thing_is_named/shadow:
       net/http: request canceled (Client.Timeout exceeded while awaiting headers)
3  [2017-07-20T10:01:58.006Z][ERROR]-sync_manager.go:375,Failed to execute sync operation {
       what_the_thing_is_named VersionDiscontinued []}"
```

A possible fix is to configure the amount of time your Greengrass core device waits for a host response. Open the greengrass-root/config/config.json file and add a system.shadowSyncTimeout field with a timeout value in seconds. For example:

```
1  {
2    "coreThing": {
3      "caPath": "root-ca.pem",
4      "certPath": "cloud.pem.crt",
```

```
 5      "keyPath": "cloud.pem.key",
 6      "thingArn": "arn:aws:iot:us-west-2:049039099382:thing/GGTestGroup42_Core",
 7      "iotHost": "your-AWS-IoT-endpoint",
 8      "ggHost": "greengrass.iot.us-west-2.amazonaws.com",
 9      "keepAlive": 600
10    },
11    "runtime": {
12      "cgroup": {
13        "useSystemd": "yes"
14      }
15    },
16    "system": {
17      "shadowSyncTimeout": 10
18    }
19  }
```

If no shadowSyncTimeout value is specified in the config.json file, the default is 1 second.

[GGC v1.1.0]

If there is a significant delay in communication between a Greengrass core device and the cloud, then shadow synchronization may fail due to a timeout. You may see something like this in your log files:

```
1  [2017-07-20T10:01:58.006Z][ERROR]-cloud_shadow_client.go:57,Cloud shadow client error: unable to
       get cloud shadow what_the_thing_is_named for synchronization. Get https://1234567890abcd.
       iot.us-west-2.amazonaws.com:8443/things/what_the_thing_is_named/shadow: net/http: request
       canceled (Client.Timeout exceeded while awaiting headers)
2  [2017-07-20T10:01:58.006Z][WARN]-sync_manager.go:263,Failed to get cloud copy: Get https
       ://1234567890abcd.iot.us-west-2.amazonaws.com:8443/things/what_the_thing_is_named/shadow:
       net/http: request canceled (Client.Timeout exceeded while awaiting headers)
3  [2017-07-20T10:01:58.006Z][ERROR]-sync_manager.go:375,Failed to execute sync operation {
       what_the_thing_is_named VersionDiscontinued []}"
```

A possible fix is to configure the amount of time your Greengrass core device waits for a host response. Open the greengrass-root/config/config.json file and add a system.shadowSyncTimeout field with a timeout value in seconds. For example:

```
 1  {
 2    "coreThing": {
 3      "caPath": "root-ca.pem",
 4      "certPath": "cloud.pem.crt",
 5      "keyPath": "cloud.pem.key",
 6      "thingArn": "arn:aws:iot:us-west-2:049039099382:thing/GGTestGroup42_Core",
 7      "iotHost": "your-AWS-IoT-endpoint",
 8      "ggHost": "greengrass.iot.us-west-2.amazonaws.com",
 9      "keepAlive": 600
10    },
11    "runtime": {
12      "cgroup": {
13        "useSystemd": "yes"
14      }
15    },
16    "system": {
17      "shadowSyncTimeout": 10
```

```
18    }
19 }
```

If no shadowSyncTimeout value is specified in the config.json file, the default is 1 second.

[GGC v1.0.0]

Not supported.

---

www.ingramcontent.com/pod-product-compliance
Lightning Source LLC
LaVergne TN
LVHW082038050326
832904LV00005B/231